Cover Your Assets

• •

Building and Managing Secure Internet Applications

Troy T. Schumaker, CISSP

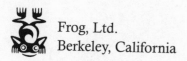
Frog, Ltd.
Berkeley, California

Riskology, Englewood, Colorado

Published by Frog, Ltd. and
Riskology, Inc.
6400 S. Fiddler's Creek Circle
Suite 2000
Englewood, Colorado 80111
www.riskology.net

Frog, Ltd. books are distributed by
North Atlantic Books
P.O. Box 12327
Berkeley, California 94712

Cover design by Linda Petrie
Book design by Paula Morrison

Printed in the United States of America

North Atlantic Books' publications are available through most bookstores. For further information, call 800-337-2665 or visit our website at www.northatlanticbooks.com.

Substantial discounts on bulk quantities are available to corporations, professional associations, and other organizations. For details and discount information, contact our special sales department.

Library of Congress Cataloging-in-Publication Data

Schumaker, Troy, 1963–
    Cover your assets : a framework for designing, implementing, deploying, and managing secure Internet applications / by Troy Schumaker and Demetrios Lazarikos.
        p. cm.
Includes bibliographical references.
    ISBN 1-58394-073-1 (pbk.)
1. Computer networks—Security measures. I. Lazarikos, Demetrios, 1968– II. Title.
TK5105.59.S38 2002
005.8—dc21
                                                           2002014711

1 2 3 4 5 6 7 8 9 / 07 06 05 04 03 02

Cover Your Assets

Good luck
coding!
Jerry

With the
Best

Table of Contents

Preface by Derk Norton

Numerous books have been written addressing the broad topic of computer and network security. Although most focus on technical details of how specific encryption and authentication techniques work, and more recently, on nontechnical security risks such as "social engineering," they do not provide a practical, well-defined path toward establishing and verifying a secure computer-application environment. My experience over the past decade as an enterprise application architect has illustrated this fact very clearly to me.

You must view the security of your enterprise applications from a holistic perspective, taking into account not only the computer systems and networks that make up your enterprise but also the people responsible for the development, deployment, and operation of those systems. Security risks can unknowingly (or even knowingly) be introduced by any number of people filling different roles in this process. This book was written to help address this aspect of the holistic approach to security.

Cover Your Assets provides a security framework, including a set of detailed security checklists targeted for the various roles within your enterprise, from executive management to operations personnel. The checklists codify the technical and process oriented security items for which each role should be responsible and held accountable. They provide me with an excellent framework within which I can judge how well the various roles within my enterprise are doing to protect our corporate assets. They can do the same for you and your enterprise.

The targeted checklists represent only half the holistic approach to security, however. Simply educating your personnel about security risks and implementing sound security policies usually is not enough to guarantee that your systems are indeed acceptably secure. An objective third-party auditing firm such as Riskology^SM should be brought in to analyze and attempt to break your security measures. They can provide a detailed report of the strengths and weaknesses of your current enterprise systems and recommend appropriate countermeasures to deal with the risks at a fraction of the cost of a typical security breach. But even if you are not ready to spend the money on a full security audit, I highly recommend this book as a first step to securing your enterprise and protecting your corporate assets.

Derk Norton, President
Pervasive Technology Group, Inc.
Louisville, Colorado

Foreword by Paul W. Cowley

Web services have dramatically changed the way an enterprise can do business. Traditionally, customers visit a physical business location to browse, gather information, purchase and pay for merchandise and services. To reach targeted markets, businesses had to locate in multiple areas. Multiple locations required redundant investments in hard and soft infrastructure. Mail order and phone order operations evolved to extend business to additional markets. However, these evolutions still were limited to market and flexibility.

Web services create a 24 by 7 virtual enterprise that can extend to the entire world via the Internet. This virtual business can be conducted with reduced need for infrastructure and costs associated with multiple physical locations. Web servers facilitate true e-business as customers can inquire about, purchase and pay for goods or services in "real time." Web services can facilitate e-commerce with other Web services. Web services can be used to enhance company image, provide information, and facilitate customer service. The extent of web services is limited only by the company's imagination.

A Web server creates a "window" into the company's information resources. The entire Internet has the potential to look into this window. Most visitors are content to legitimately browse or utilize the services provided on the Web site. However, there are those who will try to pry open the window and gain access to non-public information, divert company information resources for their own needs, deface the company's Web site or disable all or part of the company's network.

The number of individuals with the technical ability to develop successful hacks against Web servers and sites is relatively small. However, successful hacks are published on hacker bulletin boards almost in "real time." Many Web site hacking exploits have been automated and the software is available on hacking sites all over the world. Today, a vulnerable Web site may be compromised or disabled by individuals with minimal technical skills from anywhere in the world.

The results of a hack against a vulnerable Web server environment can range from annoying to disastrous. A company's image or public relations could be adversely affected by the defacement of its Web site. Information technology resources (or actual goods and services) could be diverted for the hacker's benefit. Those same information resources could be used to attack an innocent third party or the company itself. Proprietary data or customers' personal and private information may be stolen or destroyed. Companies that would never allow an unauthorized individual physical access to their inventory, administrative or operational records may inadvertently allow such cyber access through vulnerabilities associated with Web services.

The goal of a Web site is to provide the access to specific data or functions utilizing the Internet. This access must be controlled to ensure the integrity of the Web services and the company's information resources. It may also include the presumption that data being exchanged and processed is confidential or private. An effective security solution will require the integration of policies and technical solutions from a variety of technology and business areas. For example, inadequate security policies will impede the creation of integrate security solutions and result in a variety of legal exposures. A properly configured firewall can be neutralized by a poorly configured Web server and vice versa. A Web application with security "bugs" can negate the security effectiveness of a properly configured Web server. Inadequate Web server design could compromise other resources in a company's network. Information that is presumed to be confidential may be compromised by insecure communications protocols over the Internet or storage on the Web server.

The authors of this publication recognize the security risks inherent in Web site/server environments. They provide an integrated approach to ensure Web-based security solutions are effective and cost-efficient. This publication provides a security framework and technical roadmap by which technicians, operations and management can design, construct, operate and manage secure Web services.

Paul W. Cowley
Director of Corporate Assurance Services
Galileo International

Foreword by Doug Tschudy

Workplace security often is given low priority. Business drivers dictate the pace, and in the midst of establishing a new Internet application or maintaining a large computing infrastructure with limited staff, the time and resources to secure them are not factored in. Administrators tasked with securing their systems and networks focus on ensuring the highest degree of reliability and performance. Although they may have created and rolled out their systems with some degree of security in mind, generally it was not the first priority, nor is it comprehensive in scope. Additionally, compromises to initial security steps are requested by internal customers who prefer elevated permissions to address a time-critical business requirement. These situations are commonplace and rarely get revisited due to the dynamic and rapid pace of the business environment. As a result, security weaknesses lie dormant and are never noticed until after an exploit as occurred.

Establishing a partnership with a qualified third-party security firm such as Riskology is essential. It provides an objective viewpoint from a resource whose sole business is security, as opposed to that of a system administrator who may regard security as a peripheral responsibility. Such a security firm brings an unbiased eye to a security review of the computing environment, identifying unseen weaknesses and areas that may benefit from additional scrutiny.

Security awareness should be a company-wide initiative and an objective for everyone in your organization. When presented with real-world examples, employees are surprised to learn how easy it is to compromise security in place with simple social engineering tactics. Security-awareness training sessions implemented on a regular basis focuses employees on their ability to contribute to the securing of the company assets and facilitates communication among functionally disparate groups.

This book is a practical guide to identifying and eliminating common security risks, establishing sound security policies, developing secure Web-based applications, and raising security awareness throughout the organization.

The incredible growth of the Internet as a business medium has been matched by the proliferation of attempts to gain unauthorized access, purloin corporate data assets, or render sites inoperable through denial-of-service attacks or viruses. Attacks range in sophistication and purpose from benign to malignant. Many IT professionals are surprised to learn that tools to exploit and gain access to supposedly secure systems are readily available for download on the Internet. These tools used to be crafted only by individuals knowledgeable in system and protocol design. Now many of these tools are available with well-packaged graphical interfaces and can be run by relative novices known as "script kiddies." The danger of corporate espionage has become more sophisticated and now has been joined by that of bored young vandals with the ability to wreak havoc on systems. The cost impact to business is staggering. Security is not a commodity to be purchased, but an ongoing process that begins with many of the steps outlined in this book and continues with ongoing vigilance.

Doug Tschudy, Technical Director
Systems & Network Security

The Need for Secure Internet-Based Applications

· ·

The dramatic rise in e-business initiatives coupled with the advent of Internet-based applications is driving unprecedented demand for applications that effectively meet business goals securely. Internet-based applications *are* the business, yet the sheer number of risks confronting these applications has never been greater.

Cover Your Assets (*CYA*) is an e-business security manual. It addresses every level of the enterprise, from senior manager to help-desk personnel. It provides a comprehensive plan to educate personnel, safeguard applications, and create a secure environment through a series of recommended polices and procedures for every team member.

The weakest link in any security chain is the people. *CYA* offers a strategic approach to building a team concept for meeting security challenges throughout the organization. Historically, e-businesses have been split between engineering and business, with security viewed primarily as an engineering concern. An environment in which the right hand does not know what the left hand is doing cannot serve an organization trying to build and maintain secure assets. This manual offers specific measures in the form of comprehensive checklists to ensure that each team member understands and executes their role in protecting key assets. Every facet of an organization must be committed to securing Internet-based applications. *CYA* fortifies existing business models by identifying both tangible and intangible assets that need protection.

On the technical side, *CYA* shows you how to develop a security plan tailored to your application needs and the size of your Web site. It offers recommendations for existing and new applications and outlines specific plans for establishing effective policies and procedures that protect those applications. *CYA* guides you through the steps to lock down your tangible assets and suggests tools to prevent, detect, and react to potential security challenges. It analyzes quality assurance and takes you through the verification process. It even tells you how to safeguard the physical plant and meet the challenge of "social engineers" trying to sweet-talk their way to sensitive information. For business-side novices, an extensive glossary clearly defines all key terms. For experienced technical hands, an annotated bibliography lists additional resources for further research.

This book is the result of forty years of combined experience in applications security. We run and operate a company that specializes in the IT security needs of small companies, large corporations, municipalities, and government agencies. We have seen the principles and procedures recommended in this book tested under fire and know they work when combined with sufficient desire. As Pogo the cartoon 'possum once said, "We have met the enemy, and he is us." We can work harder, or we can get smarter. Use the information in this e-business security manual, and you can protect your job, your assets, and your company's future.

Welcome to the Wild Wild Web

How bad has it gotten out there? Consider the following statistics noted in recent security journals:

- The Web site www.attrition.org, whose sole charter was to track Web-site defacements simply gave up at the end of May 2001 because the volunteer staff could no longer *keep up with the volume.*

- By causing an estimated $2.6 billion in damages to 300,000 infected computers, Code Red was the biggest virus of 2001. It spread by exploiting a known vulnerability in servers running Microsoft's Internet Information Services (IIS) Web software.

• It has been proven that within days of placing an unannounced Web server on the public Internet thousands of people will be hacking away at it.

Clearly, the Internet no longer provides a secured operating environment for production applications.

The Security Jigsaw Puzzle

Forty years ago, in the midst of the Cold War, John F. Kennedy issued one of the nation's most stirring calls to duty in a new era of shared responsibility: "Ask not what your country can do for you, ask what you can do for your country." In the realm of e-business, the task of maintaining the security of key assets doesn't just happen; everyone in the organization needs to ask themselves what they can do to take an active role. Like a jigsaw puzzle, all the pieces of a security strategy must be in place to form a complete picture, and everyone in the company holds a piece to the security puzzle. In the following pages we analyze the components of this security puzzle, spelling out principles and guidelines for each area of responsibility.

To provide secure Internet-based applications, individuals within an organization collectively must apply all the principles involved. Each of the "Guiding Principles" listed at the end of each team-member description and elsewhere throughout this book provides a key piece of the security puzzle. The sum of these parts is sustainable security. Read and absorb these principles, meditate on them, and apply them in your day-to-day roles.

The Foundation
of Secure Internet Applications

Secure Internet-based applications are based on three fundamental areas of security:

- *Confidentiality* of information
- *Integrity* of information
- *Availability* of information

Maintaining Confidentiality

Maintaining confidentiality ensures that only authorized individuals or computer processes *gain access to secure information.* Keeping information confidential is a critical goal, but accomplishing this goal is more easily said than done.

The primary means of maintaining confidentiality is through *authentication*—the process of confirming the identity of a particular subject or object before allowing it access to information. Authentication confirms that a user is certified to be who he or she claims to be. Typically, Internet-based applications provide authentication mechanisms in the form of a username and/or password identification, although more sophisticated technology may be applied in the form of biometric authentication or digital certificates.

A secondary means of maintaining confidentiality is through *access control*—the process of limiting information access to authorized individuals or objects. Access control and authentication work hand in hand by (1) providing access only after a user's authentication has been confirmed and (2) by limiting the information to which that user may gain access.

To illustrate this two-step process, take the example of logging onto a computer and bringing up a specific document in a text editor. The authentication process consists of logging into the computer by entering a username and password. This information is sent to a database for verification, and if the information is verified, you are logged into the system. Next, you try to bring up a specific document to read. The access control mechanism surveys the security permissions for that particular file and decides according to a series of parameters whether you are permitted to view that file. By allowing or denying read access to the file, the access control system does its job by maintaining the confidentiality of the information.

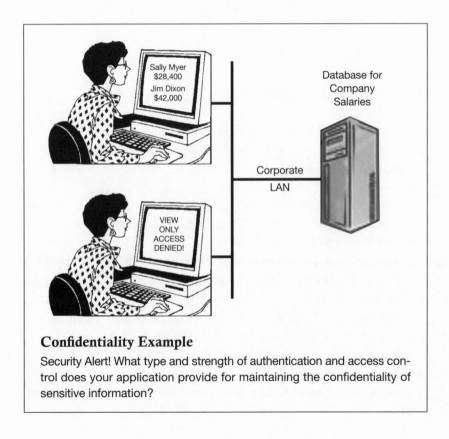

Confidentiality Example

Security Alert! What type and strength of authentication and access control does your application provide for maintaining the confidentiality of sensitive information?

Maintaining System Integrity

Maintaining system integrity ensures that *only authorized individuals or objects* have access to change secure information. Again, access control provides the primary means for maintaining integrity. Where confidentiality ensures that information is viewed only by authorized entities, integrity ensures that information is *updated and/or deleted only by authorized entities.*

Take the example of our user logging into the system and viewing a text file. If he tries to go one step further and modify the file, the access control mechanism would require authorization for this event. Imagine logging onto a system and increasing your salary any time you felt the urge. What if your bank could transfer money out of your checking account any time it wanted? It is easy to see the need for effective system integrity.

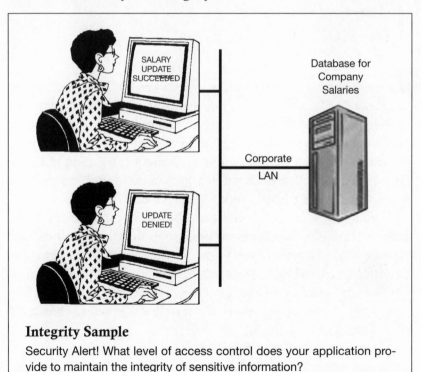

Integrity Sample

Security Alert! What level of access control does your application provide to maintain the integrity of sensitive information?

Necessary Audit Trails

An audit trail is an automated or manual set of records that provides documentary evidence of user transactions. What level of audit trail does your application provide? Is it sufficient to track down anomalies and unauthorized accesses?

Typically an Internet-based application contains numerous log files to capture the sequence of events in an e-commerce transaction. These may include both informational and error messages. Log files can be drawn from a number of different sources, including but not limited to:

- Web server
- Database server
- Application server
- Operating system
- Firewall
- Router

Log files are vital for tracking down errors or security breaches; an audit trail documents log files for specific functions or transactions by providing date and time in a form that cannot be forged or modified. Because an audit trail may be produced as evidence in a court of law, its accuracy and inviolability are critical. Frequently, audit trails use digital signatures that essentially "sign" an audit trail in a manner that keeps someone from tampering with it at a later date.

The log file and audit trail have different purposes, even if one does not take the extra steps required to "sign" the audit trail. Log files, which are larger, are used for troubleshooting the sequence of an e-commerce transaction. Audit trails contain records of all business transactions, whether they have been completed or aborted. Log files may be selectively turned on or off ("throttled"), whereas audit trails should always be on.

Organizations should closely examine their audit trail policy to determine who is responsible for providing the audit trail in the likely event of a security breach. An audit trail needs to be stored off-site on a long-term basis to remain available for legal reasons to provide the details of past transactions stemming from your company's Internet-based applications.

Providing Availability

The final area fundamental to IS security is availability—*the timely and reliable access to data and information services for authorized users.* When you decide to log onto your banking application, you assume that it is going to be up and working in a timely fashion. Availability provides "up time" for your users. It does not matter how secure your application is, if your users cannot access it, they lose time, and you lose money.

To maintain availability, one must consider:

• Scalability

• Failover

• Data replication

• Identifying points of failure

Scalability

No one likes a slow application. It wastes user time and suggests inefficiency and incompetence. Providing acceptable performance is a discipline in itself. The rule of thumb for maintaining timely performance is that two Web servers outperform one, four outperform two, and so on. By closely monitoring the usage of all devices in your application and increasing the scale as needed, you can make prudent capital equipment expenditures that give each of your users the impression that the application is responding in a timely manner.

Failover

Count on Murphy's Law. Any piece of equipment can and will fail at some point. Providing redundant Web servers ensures that, should one Web server fail, another will be available, thus providing users with the appearance of 24/7 up time. Although the application may slow slightly because it is running on one less Web server, the application is still available to perform e-business.

Data Replication

Providing timely backups for all of your production systems can save you time rebuilding systems that need to come online rapidly. Although the database server typically will be your primary concern, all systems should have regularly scheduled backups. Finally, regularly scheduled "restores" of backups should be performed offline. How else can you verify your backups?

Identifying Single Points of Failure

To maintain availability, identify all single points of failure, define a plan for redundancy, and implement the plan. The following elements comprise the main areas of concern.

Hardware: Have you provided redundancy for each of the physical devices comprising your Web site? What would happen if the corporate firewall device suddenly stopped working? Do you have a spare?

Software: What will you do if the operating system fails? Does a standard operating procedures manual exist that describes all steps required to rebuild the system? These include:

- Where to find the CD
- How to install the operating system
- How to reinstall applications

Network: What policies and procedures are in place for dealing with a denial-of-service (DoS) attack? Prevention is the best medicine, but even with the best prevention, security is not an exact science.

Application: Is it well distributed? If a database server crashes and the application must reconnect to another working database server, is it resilient enough to do so seamlessly?

Roles and Responsibilities— The Human Dimension

• •

The hardware and software mechanisms that maintain confidentiality, integrity, and availability of sensitive information are only as good as the human team members configuring and monitoring them. Are you doing everything in your power to ensure that your team can reach these goals?

When breaches arise, team members are often unclear about their role in the security puzzle. It was often said of the great Boston Celtic basketball player Bill Russell that he knew where every player was on the court at any given moment. To play your role, you must know what your responsibilities are and how you fit in the larger scheme. You may not be a senior manager, but when you understand her responsibilities, you can anticipate her needs. Here are the players:

- Senior Management
- Security Director
- Director (or Program Manager)
- Operations Manager
- Operations Team
- Technical Leader
- Technical Team

As you read through job descriptions and the guiding principles for each team member, keep in mind your role and responsibilities in relation to them. It is wiser to work smarter than harder. Greater awareness yields better security.

Senior Manager

As senior manager, you hold fiduciary responsibility for the company. You set policies that maximize return on assets and operations while reducing liabilities. In addition to its tangible valuations, the company's reputation is also your charge, along with the trust and confidence of clients and shareholders.

The security of the company's Internet-based applications should be among your primary concerns. If you do not support security initiatives loudly and clearly, security will never be perceived as important. Employees will become lax in carrying out security initiatives, and in the end most security initiatives will fail.

As senior manager, you must understand all the security risks facing the organization. You must be kept well informed of these risks, and in turn make prudent security decisions on behalf of the company. Failure to build secure systems leads to increased costs for the organization. Why omit important security principles now when they will most likely surface later?

Security decisions should be made after closely reviewing the risk analysis prepared by the security director's staff and/or a third-party security auditor.

Losses associated with security breaches include the following:

Loss of Reputation

Bad press in any form damages a company, and nothing is as embarrassing as receiving bad press due to exploited Internet-based applications. Such incidents can reduce client confidence and send them looking for alternatives your competitors may provide. It can take years to build a company's reputation; do not let a security breach tear it down in a few moments.

Online computer and software retailer Egghead.com's reputation was shattered when a security flaw in its e-commerce software was exploited by hackers who stole roughly 3.7 million credit-card numbers from the company's servers. Egghead customers left in droves after being notified of the theft, and shares of the company's stock fell to as low as $0.50 after trading as high as $13.50.—*Computerworld Security Watch,* December 22, 2000

Loss of Revenue

It is difficult to calculate the tangible and intangible impact of implementing security fixes; nevertheless, the Microsoft Security Response Center estimates that a security bulletin-based bug costs $100,000.

> Customers of popular tax preparation website e1040.com were preparing to sue after their private information—including passwords and Social Security numbers—was displayed in plain text on the Internet due to a switching error in the site's encryption software.—CNET News.com, February 12, 2001

Conventional wisdom suggests that the greatest return on investment (ROI) is reaped when the organization *proactively* builds secure applications!

Guiding Principles

As the driving force behind enterprise-wide security awareness and security initiatives, your actions make or break the organization. Your actions always speak louder than words. In today's e-business climate, business concerns are more important than technical issues. Key decisions about software development and deployment are no longer exclusively the province of the IT department. Because Internet-based applications are important to the company's overall well-being, senior management must play a central role in all business-critical decisions, including the design and development of e-business applications.

- Recognize that successful e-business strategies are grounded in secure Internet-based applications.
- Actively manage risk factors. Know the variables associated

with application risk management and how they impact the overall risk equation.

- Think of application risk management in terms of business objectives. Learn and understand which risks to ignore and which to address.

- Think of security as an ongoing process, not as a product. Just because the organization has a firewall, that does not mean the network is absolutely secure.

- Deploy risk management not only for in-house applications, but for outsourced applications, as well, such as acquiring and integrating off-the-shelf/freeware components.

- Have a sound set of policies and procedures that the organization can learn and follow. (Read more on this in Chapter 3, "Policies and Procedures.")

- Revise the annual performance review to include incentives for employees who uncover risks to the organization. Financial reward can be a strong motivator for the way people think and act about security.

Security Director

You command all security initiatives. You set the example for providing a secure operating environment. You are the administrating intelligence behind the organization's security posture. In addition, you are responsible for collecting all forms of input concerning vulnerabilities and liabilities. Based on this information, you will prioritize and implement security programs that maintain a tight security posture.

As security director, you must address the following concerns:

- Are the organization's policies and procedures sufficient?

- Are the policies and procedures utilized in the day-to-day workplace?

- How secure are the applications currently in production?

- How can the organization design applications to operate safely amidst current threats and vulnerabilities while anticipating future concerns?
- What critical security challenges confront the organization?
- How do I distill the array of security threats and volumes of risk-management literature into an effective roadmap that can protect the business at all times?
- When was the last comprehensive risk analysis performed on an enterprise level? What programs have been instituted to address the highest risks it revealed?

Once you have identified weak links within the organization and its applications, you will direct others to address these concerns. This requires the ability to communicate with others and to educate them about the risks, as well as to motivate increased participation in addressing and managing those risks across the enterprise.

Guiding Principles

- Engage in security discussions with as many people as possible both inside and outside the organization. Listen to everyone in the organization, not just senior management.
- Praise team members for their initiatives. Educate the organization about the risks, liabilities, and consequences of weak security.
- Manage the risks stated in the risk analysis by applying a variety of countermeasures.
- Monitor the agreed-upon countermeasures.
- Think about security as an ongoing process, instead of a product. A firewall does not make a network absolutely secure.
- Provide ongoing security awareness training for the entire organization.

Director or Program Manager

You are the linchpin between senior management goals and the teams that actually build, deploy, and manage e-business applications. Your security perspective is also multidirectional. In overseeing the security of key assets, you should carry the security flag that senior management has declared paramount to the success of the business. Educate and mentor the teams who implement your reports in this area. You also must provide feedback to the security director (and/or senior managers) from the team members who report to you. Finally, a director or program manager oversees the security of key assets in every facet of production or deployment from project inception to completion, whether its life cycle is measured in weeks, months, or years.

Guiding Principles

- As security mediator connecting the needs of senior management to operations, your feedback is critical to management decision-making, and your example determines team motivation and desire to increase the organization's overall security posture. If you act as if security is not important, your teams soon will follow suit. Should you make security a top priority, however, your teams will shortly subscribe to that example.

- Praise your team members for their security initiatives. Build in incentives to increase their awareness of security concerns.

- Don't get caught up in adding more and more features without adhering to the security needs of the application. Security requirements are by definition among an application's most important features. Factor them into the project schedule from the start.

16

Operations Manager

An operations manager oversees the day-to-day security concerns confronting the company's Internet-based applications. Your role is critical in providing ongoing shields to protect production-system confidentiality, integrity, and availability.

In addition to supervising security patches, operating-system upgrades, application upgrades, firewall rules, and backups, you are in a key position to mentor the team that does this work on a daily basis. You are responsible for its morale and performance. Additional cyber-threats have no doubt increased the workload for you and your team, but you can pride yourselves in the fact that you are the front line of defense in providing operational security for the company's Internet-based applications.

Guiding Principles

- Work closely with the security director on key decisions such as when to apply security patches, or when and how to reconfigure the firewall rules. Open channels to your security director ensure a well-balanced implementation of the company's security initiatives.

- Praise team members for their initiatives. Create incentives to reward their attention to and creativity in addressing security concerns.

- Regularly monitor all log files (for all devices) for intrusions. Utilize tools to help out in this arduous task.

- Less is more: Simplify the production environment to reduce security risks.

- Be aware of disgruntled operations employees who may be in a position to inflict damage.

Operations Team Member

As an operations team member, you are the eyes and ears monitoring security for the company's Internet-based applications moment by moment. You act as sentry to protect production-system confidentiality, integrity, and availability.

In addition to applying security patches, upgrading operations, and changing firewall rules to support new business needs, you must keep abreast of the latest security threats and the state-of-the-art technologies that deal with those threats. (This alone can be an exhausting task.)

Nevertheless, as with any IT operations team, your role in maintaining production systems is the lifeline of the company's revenue stream.

Guiding Principles

- Remember, technology is not a cure-all for security. Your role is to be vigilant. Follow prudent security policies and procedures to ensure that production systems are locked down.
- Think of security as an ongoing process, not a one-time product. A firewall cannot guarantee security. Do not be led to believe that cryptography alone can secure an Internet-based application.
- Your responsibility is enormous. You have access to the company's key assets. Be on guard against social engineering attacks.

Technical Leader

As a tech lead, you are a mentor to your fellow developers. Your role is critical in motivating developers to think about security on a daily basis. It is not enough to inculcate a generalized concern; you must educate your team members about the multitude of security issues surrounding design and implementation. Ultimately you direct the implementation of authentication, access control, and audit trails, while ensuring high availability of the application.

Make your team members curious. Encourage them to educate themselves about security issues. Start a "brown-bag" lunch program: Every month, assign each member to read at least one publication related to the field of developing secure applications. At the end of the month, over lunch, each team member shares an overview of key principles from their reading, as well as specific areas in which this new information can be applied to benefit the company's current development methodologies.

Consider outsourcing formal training sessions on how to avoid potential security pitfalls in designing and implementing applications (buffer overflows and the like).

Guiding Principles

- Work closely with the security director, program manager, and operations manager to survey authentication, access control, audit trails and high availability. Your developers may have the ability to build cool features into an application, but often they do not know how to design or build in security modules necessary to support authentication and access control.

- Praise your developers for their hard work and interest in building secure applications.

- Keep abreast of the latest methodologies for the design and implementation of secure applications. (Refer to the Annotated Bibliography included at the end of this book for recommended reading on this topic.)

- Subscribe to security-alert email lists. Simply receiving and reading these on a daily basis will heighten your awareness of the need for secure applications.

- Beware of disgruntled technical employees who are in a prime position to steal and/or vandalize.

Technical Team Member

As a developer you are a "top gun" who can revitalize a company with innovative new offerings or send it belly up with careless oversights. For a developer, life is a constant battle to stay on the cutting edge. You must keep ahead of the array of features going into the next release of the product, while mastering the latest methodologies surrounding the design and implementation of secure Internet-based applications.

It is your job to anticipate hackers, know more than the enemy, and be better informed about every aspect of security surrounding the applications you are developing. You do not want to learn that the company's Web site just got hacked, and the heat is on *you* to figure out what happened, fix it, and make sure it cannot happen again.

Guiding Principles

- You cannot tack on security at the end of a beta program. It must be a primary concern from the very first design meeting. Developers typically can build "cool" features into an application, but often do not know how to design or build the required security modules that support authentication and access control.

- Keep abreast of the latest methodologies for designing and implementing secure applications. (Refer to the Annotated Bibliography included at the end of this book for recommended reading on this topic.)

- Subscribe to security-alert email lists. Simply receiving and reading these on a daily basis will heighten your awareness of the need for secure applications.

- Think about security as a process, not a product. Firewalls and cryptography are not enough to secure an application, especially for components that are accessible directly from the Internet.

Policies and Procedures

•••

Too often the expression "policies and procedures" brings to mind a white binder parked on a dusty shelf full of outdated technical manuals. If you should ask anyone in your organization for "Policies and Procedures" and they direct you to that binder, you will know it is time to develop a new suite of policies that address every conceivable security contingency.

The following sections identify each area of your organization that a policy should cover.

Enterprise-Wide Security Policies and Procedures

•••

An enterprise-wide security policies-and-procedures document should address all areas of concern related to protecting the company's intellectual property, IT assets, physical assets, and employee safety. Each policy should be succinct. A well-written policy statement never exceeds two pages. Anyone should be able to read and understand it in five minutes. Period.

In developing security policies and procedures, senior management should include the following action items:

• Organize a Security Council that will create, vote on, distribute, and monitor all policies and procedures for the organization. Invite individuals from sales, marketing, operations, software development, and business development, as well as several members from senior management to sit on the Council (e.g., this way, policy acceptance will be much greater since each division has had input as well as buy-in to the policies and procedures.)

• Provide a complete document that defines all prudent security policies and procedures for the company.

• Assign policy ownership explicitly to one or more individuals (policy owners). The policy should be posted on the company's Intranet for easy access and updating.

• Demand mandatory policy compliance by all individuals in the company. Require every officer and employee of the company to read, understand, sign, and fully agree to comply with the security policies and procedures.

• Conduct policy audits annually, including a review by all senior management and policy owners. Annual reviews may result in keeping the policy intact, amending it, or possibly deleting the policy altogether.

If the last step does not take place, your company may well repeat history, with everyone pointing to the white binder on the dusty shelf.

Appendix I of this book provides a sample security policy and procedure outline. It is straightforward and highlights all areas of concern that must be addressed prior to tackling Internet-based application security.

Privacy Policies

Privacy policies notify Web site users of the extent to which the confidentiality of their personally identifiable information will be protected. It spells out how information will be used and shared.

Today's Internet-based applications must take the high road when addressing concerns about how subscriber information is used and shared. Although there has been a recent shift in priorities from privacy to security, every organization should provide a privacy policy on the company's corporate Web site disclosing to clients the following privacy information:

- The information collected (name, age, email address, and so on)
- How it is collected (are cookies utilized?)
- How personally identifiable information is used (for example, to market products back to the client)
- Whether this information is shared or sold to other businesses and, if so, to whom, and how. Does the client have a means to control this? If so, how?
- How secure the collected information is; for example, when a credit card is used, does the Web site reveal only the last five digits? And what type of authentication mechanisms does the site provide? Does it require that a password include more than four characters?
- The personally identifiable information, including account information, that can be accessed
- Client options for removal from email campaigns

In addition to disclosing to clients how their information is to be used and shared, the privacy policy also defines security features in the application. For example, will the application use secure connections when transmitting personally identifiable information? Will the application provide a mechanism in the form of a Web page to allow users to update their mailing addresses?

Guiding Principles

- The privacy policy should be easy to read and understand.
- It should reflect accurately the measures your Web site provides to protect the confidentiality of your client's personally identifiable information.

Terms-of-Use Statement

In addition to a privacy policy, each Web site should include a terms- (or conditions-) of-use statement. Disclosures made in the terms of use are legal in nature and override anything stated in the privacy policy,

23

although in theory they should be consistent. A growing trend is to make users take an active role in accepting the terms of use. This not only mitigates legal risk from the company's perspective, but proactively involves the user with the rules of the given Web site.

Terms of use should disclose the following legal bodies of knowledge:

- Copyright
- Trademarks
- Patents
- License and site access
- User account information
- Risk of loss
- Product descriptions
- Disclaimer of warranties and limitation of liability
- Applicable law
- Disputes
- Site policies

Have your organization's legal counsel review and approve the terms-of-use statement. It is one of the most important legal documents your company discloses publicly.

Bill of Rights

Another new trend in privacy policies is the client/customer's "bill of rights." One of the world's most popular Web sites, www.amazon.com, offers a bill of rights in addition to their privacy policy and terms-of-use statement. The Amazon Bill of Rights makes five policy statements that includes rights the client/customer visiting their site may take for granted.

1. The customer's credit card safety is protected.

2. The customer is under no obligation to make a purchase.

3. The customer may unsubscribe or change his/her subscription at any time.

4. The customer will occasionally receive updates, but can change his/her preferences.

5. The customer may access the privacy policy, which describes the information collected, how that information is used, and the choices the client customer has with respect to that information.

Clearly, a bill of rights provides *additional reassurance* to customers and further allays their fears of engaging in online credit-card transactions.

Guiding Principles

- Design and implement a bill of rights for your Web site.
- Stand behind it.

Handling Variances in Policy

In a perfect world, all policies and procedures would be implemented with 100 percent accuracy and timeliness. In the real world, often this is not the case. Nevertheless, the goal should be to implement policies and execute their procedures as quickly and precisely as possible.

When a situation arises demanding a variance in policy, this should be brought to the attention of the Security Council. (Remember, every policy has one.) The owner will discuss the variance and decide whether to accept or reject it. In most cases there will be tolerable variances.

When an acceptable variance has been identified, the following should occur:

1. The Security Council should make an addendum to the policy stating the variance.

2. The Security Council should recirculate the updated policy to all officers.

3. The Security Council should recirculate the updated policy to all employees via the corporate Intranet.

Guiding Principle

Assume up front that your policies and procedures will be flexible; after all, e-business itself is dynamic.

Threat Analysis
for E-Business Applications

As with any analysis, the goal here is to make an informed decision based on the variables in a given situation. When it comes to devising a security strategy for e-business, one must consider many factors.

The following table highlights a range of threats to an Internet-based application and countermeasures to deflect those threats.

Threat	Countermeasure	Comment
Session replay—the process of listening to and storing all HTTP requests and responses from a valid application session for later playback to gain unauthorized access to the application	Design the application to utilize secure TCP/IP connections. This may be accomplished by using either SSL/HTTPS or IPSEC.	Secure connections can slow an application, so use them judiciously (that is, only when sensitive information is flowing—for example, logging on).

(Continued on page 28)

Threat	Countermeasure	Comment
Unauthorized modification of the application's configuration files	Ensure that all Web servers, application servers and database servers are locked down with few user accounts. Run the application servers behind the firewall. Firewall the Web site from the corporate LAN Implement intrusion-detection systems in your network security to detect common denial-of-service attacks.	By implementing a firewall from the internal LAN, unauthorized access to the internal LAN does not imply open access to the systems housing your application.
A Web-based dictionary attack "guesses" username and password	Disable the account for the username after five invalid tries. Have the application send an email or page announcing this event. Authentication module should provide an audit trail for greater than five failed login attempts (log source IP address, date, and time).	If someone cannot log onto a system within five attempts, something is suspicious. Beware of a number of programs that provide Web-based dictionary attacks on Internet-based application login pages.

Threat	Countermeasure	Comment
Email containing sensitive account information is "snooped" by unauthorized user.	Transmit account information by more secure means, such as password-protected MS-WORD document, or using digital certificates.	Never send sensitive account information across inherently insecure email.
Attacker maliciously impersonates a server	Use SSL (or IPSEC), which supports a server-authentication scheme.	
Attacker gains physical access to the server machine.	Keep server room in a separate locked facility. Keep computer screen locked. Use strong passwords and/or pass phrases. Change administrative passwords quarterly. Encrypt sensitive information (such as private keys).	Although this is less likely to occur than an electronic attack, internally caused theft and/or damage by rogue employees is not uncommon.

(Continued on page 30)

Threat	Countermeasure	Comment
Denial-of-service attack	Throttle the application (that is, if greater than MAX connections have occurred, do not allow another connection to begin a transaction). Use external monitoring products (such as SiteScope) to detect a denial-of-service condition.	Closely monitoring the application is a luxury not everyone can afford. This can aid in additional countermeasures, however, such as changing DNS entries to point to another Web server and halt the current attack. The distributed denial-of-service attack is difficult to detect. Keep your eyes on newer technologies being released to address this problem.
Accessing private, sensitive data	Lock down all Web directories to render unauthorized access impossible. Turn on access control mechanisms in Web Server. Encrypt data, if necessary, or do not store sensitive information.	Private and sensitive data generally should be placed on a company's internal network (secured behind various firewalls).

Threat	Countermeasure	Comment
Viewing sensitive information stored in the cookie	Either encrypt the information stored in the cookie or don't store sensitive information in the cookie.	Consider setting the "secure" flag on a cookie so it passes only over an HTTPS-based connection.
Unauthorized modification of the cookie	Recompare/Checksum/Sign the cookie at the server. Take appropriate action if invalid.	
Attacker attempts to post bogus scripts and/or HTML to your site.	Validate all input fields using regular expressions (look for tokens such as <HTML> or <SCRIPT>). Discard input if any of these are found.	Mitigate cross-site scripting (CSS) attacks against your Internet-based application.
Attacker attempts a buffer overflow.	Validate all input lengths to reasonable MAX lengths.	

(Continued on page 32)

Threat	Countermeasure	Comment
Attacker opens hundreds of connections to your application but does nothing with any of them.	Restrict access via authentication mechanisms. Log all valid and invalid logins to log files (including IP address). Run scripts every 1/2 hour that check log files for predefined *suspicious* activity.	

Application Security Considerations

● ●

A cyberattacker typically targets the weakest link in the security chain. This weak link may be the application software, the host operating system, or even an unwitting help-desk employee at the end of a social-engineering call.

Identifying weak links before an attacker can target them requires the skill and foresight of sound risk analysis. First, identify those risks that would incur the greatest damage. Mitigate these risks, and then move on to the next. Prioritize your weaknesses and move quickly to bolster them.

Design Security into the Application by Default

● ●

Internet-based applications—and all applications, for that matter—should strive to build all security-related features into the system as default behaviors. Security features often exist in applications, yet they are disabled by default. The problem is that users rarely enable them, because most users do not understand security issues or the need for security features in applications. Unfortunately, we know better.

A classic example of this occurs when a browser dialog box warns you when you are about to open a secure connection (for example, an SSL/HTTPS session being established by the Internet-based browser application with a remote server). This information is nice to know, but it would be far more useful if the dialog box included information about the security implications of this connection, such as:

- Encryption strength (40 bits isn't strong enough, 128 bits is sufficient)
- Certificate validity—has it been checked against a revocation list? Is it stolen?
- URL of the Web site that provided the certificate—the application could encourage the user to view the URL window and confirm that this is the same URL.

Implementing Secure Applications

To create secure applications, one must become intimately involved with the design and implementation of the authentication and access modules at the onset. Understand authentication and access modules religiously and take full advantage of implementing robust audit control modules and rich logging capabilities. Security should never be tacked on as an afterthought!

To get a system up and running, developers routinely output to an audit trail–based log file in order to track information such as "in module XYZ, function DEF." But once the system is up and running, they stop using the audit trail. To create a secure application, use the audit trail to its full capability throughout the development cycle and beyond.

The benefits of a well-designed, secure application include the following:

1. If the system should fail at production time, the application can still read from a configuration file (or registry entry) each time as it cycles, checking for a debug flag being set to true. Upon reading the value to true, the application can begin sending volumes of output to the log file, so that an understanding of what is going on can be captured easily for debugging purposes. This helps to keep the application available.

2. Input validation routines, which check for lengths to avoid buffer

overflows, send output to the logging routines. When the developers of the application patch up the exploit, often they put additional audit trails around the code with statements such as "It looks someone's trying to hack us," and log the URL, date and time, and so on. The operations team must monitor log files closely to detect changes to the application and maintain the integrity of the application.

How to Mitigate Buffer Overflows

To mitigate buffer overflows, the Internet-based application should have a well-written application programming interface (API) that supports strong input validation. This API should be heavily reviewed, tested, and reused in all production applications. The API is the application's first line of defense. *Never trust the input.*

A well-written API will:

- Check the lengths of all input. If greater than the maximum length, simply stop processing and return failure.

- Validate input type. Ideally, all input should be validated with a regular expression, therefore this validation module would accept as input a "regular expression" and the routine would return success/failure after validating it against the input stream.

- Validate input from configuration files, registry entries, command line, URL line, environment variables, and so on.

- Inhibit HTML-based input, which can open up vulnerabilities for cross-site scripting (CSS).

Validating your input is *critical* to mitigating buffer overflows.

Avoid Storing Credentials in Software

All configuration files (and/or registry entries) that contain username and password credentials should be encrypted or stored in binary format. This provides a second level of defense should your host system be compromised. If the configuration file is ASCII only and contains the ODBC/JDBC username/password credentials to the database, then anyone can guess where the unauthorized intruder will head.

Avoid Insecure Functions

Simply put, create a policy among all developers to avoid the use of common functions that are susceptible to buffer overflows, such as sprintf(), gets(), and strcpy(). Their shortcomings have been publicized for many years, yet they continue to be used. Such an oversight provides one more reason to conduct regular security-code reviews.

Digitally Sign Production Files

Make it a common practice to digitally "sign" your applications' CAB and/or JAR files. This provides the users (and your organization) with a high level of certainty that the software has not been tampered with (that is, someone has not placed a Trojan horse inside your application). A variety of third-party tools are available to facilitate such digital signatures and a number of APIs to check against those signatures.

Avoid Faulty Assumptions

You have heard it before, and you will hear it again: Think outside the box to avoid assumptions such as:

- That will never happen to us.
- It has never happened before.
- We have a firewall; we're secure. (Remember, the Code Red worm came right through the firewall using port 80, the port Web sites typically run on.)
- The input will never be greater than 50 bytes.

Assumptions like these build a false sense of security.

Run with Least Privilege

Typically, applications are run with the highest privileges, such as root, on Unix systems, or administrator privileges, on Windows platforms. Rarely is this necessary, and often it opens the door for a remote root exploit. Someone causing a buffer overflow can force the application to terminate and relinquish control back to the command that launched the application.

Instead, write your applications to run with the least necessary privilege. In the case where you absolutely need to run as root (perhaps the application must bind to a low port on a Unix machine for low-level socket reads or device driver interoperability), simply design the root process so it spawns another process with much lower privileges. Web servers work exactly like this.

Running applications with least privilege reduces the risks of fraud, theft, and vandalism of IT assets.

Application Servers

The less software you have to write, the faster your e-business applications will get to market. Save yourself time and money by leveraging the many security features inherent in today's application servers. Out of the box, these products offer the following security-related features and functions:

- *Authentication* modules
- Extensible *access control* modules
- *Auditing* modules
- Digital certificate modules

Why reinvent the wheel if you can leverage existing software?

Commercially Available Application Servers

A wide range of application servers exists on the market today. With a little research you can quickly determine which is best for your IT environment. Keep in mind, however, that if you are an Oracle-only shop, the Oracle application server may best fulfill your needs; if you are a Microsoft-based shop, chances are the .NET server will meet your requirements.

Here is a list of the most common application servers on the market today.

BEA WebLogic

http://www.bea.com/products/security/index.shtml

This Java-based application server has been on the market for nearly five years and has a rich and robust set of security-related APIs.

IBM WebSphere Application Server

http://www-3.ibm.com/software/info1/websphere/index.jsp

IBM's offering is similar to the BEA WebLogic application server.

IPlanet

http://www.sub.com/software

This Java-based application server is part of the Netscape/Sun Microsystems next generation Netscape application server.

Microsoft .NET

http://www.microsoft.com/net/default.asp

One of the most exciting recent application servers (or application environments), this one contains a wealth of APIs.

Oracle

http://www.oracle.com/ip/deploy/ias/

Oracle's offering is not quite as mature as the BEA solution, but it contains some interesting Oracle-specific features.

Chapter 6

Web-Site Security Considerations

When your team is ready to implement an Internet-based application in the form of a Web site, provide a clear sense of the project to everyone involved. Have concrete answers to the following questions:

- What is the business purpose of the Web site?
- What is the anticipated user load (that is, how many users per day)?
- How many machines will comprise the application?
- What kind of redundancy will be built into the architecture and design?
- What types of sensitive information will the Web site store?
- Where will the Web site be housed (in-house or at a collocation facility)?
- How large is the budget for this Web site?
- How much effort is involved with new software development?
- Is security being considered smart e-business and *not* a luxury?

Answering these questions can facilitate unity among the many teams that will make the Web site a success.

The following three sections address key security considerations for your Web site.

Lightweight Web Site

A lightweight Web site is purely informational. It conveys information, but it does not collect and store it. Think of a corporate Web site that describes a company's products and services. The amount of time, money, and effort required to design, build, deploy, and manage this lightweight Web site pales in comparison with the efforts associated with creating a "heavyweight" Web site, with its vast range of e-commerce services.

Security measures

- Provide an outer firewall, which allows only HTTP access (via port 80) to the Web servers.

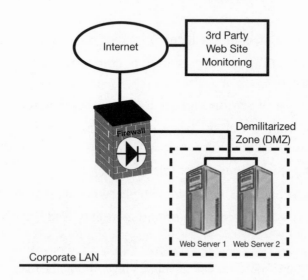

Lightweight Web Site

Figure 1. Design for a lightweight Web site. Note that the DMZ is a separate network from the corporate LAN.

- Implement a demilitarized zone (DMZ) to contain the IP addresses for the Web servers. (This is a separate and distinct network from your corporate LAN; therefore, if this machine is compromised, the corporate LAN is not.)

- Implement a firewall rule that prohibits all accesses from the Web servers into the corporate LAN, aside from a firewall rule that allows only a single port access into the corporate LAN. This port may be accessed to administer the Web site by authorized personnel (typically via either Windows Terminal Server or SSH).

- Purchase two physical machines to be used as Web servers. This way, if one of them fails, your informational Web site remains up and running.

- Lock down the operating system on these two computers. That is, disable all unnecessary accounts and services. For services that must run, set security levels to as low as possible, apply all security patches, and so on.

- Monitor the Web server log files daily to ensure that the machine is running correctly and has not been compromised.

- Run external monitoring software (for example. SiteScope) to automatically detect when one or both Web servers are down.

Middleweight Web Site

A middleweight Web site is a scaled-down version of a full-blown ("heavyweight") e-commerce Web site. It is more sophisticated than a lightweight Web site, in that it includes one or more database machines that store sensitive information (userid, password, and the like). This Web site not only conveys basic information, it keeps track of users, options, and potentially facilitates online purchases.

Security Measures

- Provide an outer firewall, which allows only HTTP/HTTPS access (via port 80/443) to the Web servers.

- Implement a firewall rule that allows only ODBC/JDBC accesses from the Web servers into the database servers on the production LAN.

- Lock down the operating system on the two database servers. That is, disable all unnecessary accounts and services. For services that must run, set security levels to as low as possible, apply all security patches, and so on.

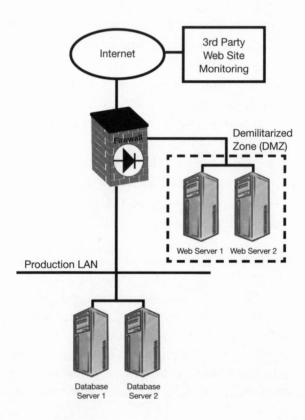

Middleweight Web Site

Figure 2. Design for a middleweight Web site. Note that the firewall allows only necessary services from the Web servers (in the DMZ) to the production database servers behind the firewall on the production LAN.

- Monitor the database server log files daily to ensure that the machine is running correctly and that it has not been compromised.

- Encrypt and store all sensitive information, such as passwords, in the database.

- Purchase redundant computers for the database servers.

Heavyweight Web Site

A heavyweight Web site offers a complete range of e-commerce services. In addition to storing sensitive information, it can process credit-card transactions while managing hundreds of thousands of user accounts and hundreds of product offerings.

Security Measures

- Use application server software running on machines separate and distinct from the Web servers'.

- Place application servers and database servers on separate networks.

- Purchase redundant computers to use as application servers.

- Lock down the operating system on the application servers. That is, disable all unnecessary accounts and services. For the services that must run, set security levels to as low as possible, apply all security patches, and so on.

- Provide a detailed audit trail.

- Consider having an entire redundant site for business continuity purposes.

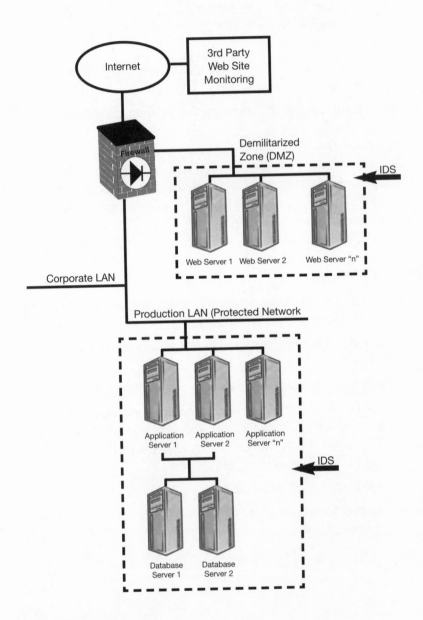

Heavyweight Web Site

Figure 3. Design for a heavyweight Web site. Note that application and database servers are not connected to the corporate LAN.

Tools to Help Monitor Security Logs

Whether or not you have a host-based IDS watching your log files, it pays to have a number of tools that help you separate the wheat from the chaff so you can tell quickly whether any suspicious activity has occurred on your production machines:

The following tools are among those currently available to help you wade through the often-voluminous log files:

- Analysis Control for Intrusion Databases (ACID), http://acidlab.sourceforge.net

- checksyslog, http://www.jammed.com/~jwa/hacks/security/checksyslog /checksyslog-doc.html

- CyberSafe Log Analyst (CLA), http://www.cybersafe.com/centrax/cla1.html

- DumpEvt, http://somarsoft.com

- Lire, http://logreport.org/lire/

- Log Analyzers, http://www.uu.se/Software/Analyzers

- PIXie, http://www.retina.net/~jna/pixie

- SeNTry ELM, http://www.serverware.com

- Security Manger, http://www.netiq.com/products/sm/default.asp

- WebTrends, http://www.netiq.com/products/sa/default.asp

Web-Server Lockdown

Regardless of what Web server you use, take the time to lock it down. For added security, take the following steps:

- Lock down the Web server with file permissions to ensure that only the Web Admin can have read/write access.

- Lock down the Web server directories so directories that contain configuration files or other sensitive information are

45

not accessible by the public accessing the Web site.

- Remove the default Web servlets and CGI scripts that were installed initially.

- Verify your work by trying to gain unauthorized access to Web pages.

- Have a third-party auditor try to gain unauthorized access to sensitive information stored on your Web site.

For those using the Microsoft IIS Web server, the Microsoft IIS lock-down tool is essential. This program (available free from Microsoft) turns off unnecessary features and accounts, thereby reducing known vulnerabilities. Visit the Microsoft Web site at http://www.microsoft.com/technet/treeview/default.asp?url=/technet/security/tools/tools/locktool.asp.

To initially (and progressively) protect your Web site, consider using a scanning tool tailored to looking for known (and unknown) vulnerabilities for that Web server. An exceptional product called WebInspect (available at www.spidynamics.com) provides a new level of protection for your critical business information.

Network Security Considerations

• •

External Shields of Defense

• •

Most Internet-based applications reside behind a router and firewall
as their external defense shields. All teams involved should understand (at some level of detail) the configuration and overall purpose
of these devices.

The process of network security requires ongoing vigilance, antic-
ipation, and problem-solving. Keep the following list of measures
and "best practices" in mind when securing and managing network
devices:

- Remove the default userid and passwords for all devices.

- Use SSH (not telnet) when configuring the device.

- Disable unnecessary services (for example, ftp, finger, telnet).

- Store passwords in a locked filing cabinet, providing access
  only to necessary personnel.

- Make regular backups of all router and firewall ACL lists and
  rules.

- Provide a backup router and firewall (in case the current one
  stops working).

- Regularly review the log files for anything suspicious.
  Identify the team member responsible for watching them.

Allocate enough time for operations personnel to review the log files (at a minimum) twice a week.

• Maintain a written procedure for handling security breaches.

• Choose strong authentication (passwords) for administrative control of all network devices. Change the passwords quarterly.

• Do not be fooled into believing that network security is the end state for a secure Internet-based application.

• Synchronize all network devices and production server clocks to be in-synch in the event that forensics are needed.

• Post an appropriately stern login banner (for example, "Unauthorized access of this resource will result in prosecution to the fullest extent of the law").

• Verify that the vendor's most recent security patches have been installed properly.

• Install intrusion-detection software (SNORT, for example).

Securing the Router

A router is a piece of equipment that acts as a traffic cop out on the Internet, telling any packets of information directed toward your organization to "get off at the next exit." Before firewalls became popular in the 1990s, routers were configured with complex access control lists (ACLs) to prevent unauthorized network traffic from traveling further downstream than the router itself. Today's complex rules authorizing and directing the flow of network traffic reside in the firewall, reducing the need for complex ACL rules. Nonetheless, it still pays to use filters on the router to stop unwanted traffic before it reaches the firewall.

Consider using these techniques to secure your router(s):

• Configure an ACL that ensures that IP spoofing rules have been configured. That is, do not allow source packets coming from the outside to have internal IP addresses. Conversely, do not allow inside packets to go out that do not have valid internal IP source addresses.

- Allow half-open sockets for no longer than roughly 10 seconds.

- Catch crash dumps, and give those files unique names for forensic purposes.

- Allow UDP to occupy no more than 2 Mb/s of the pipe.

- Allow ICMP to occupy no more than 500 Kb/s of the pipe.

- Allow multicast to occupy no more than 5 Mb/s of the pipe.

- Do not send redirects.

- Do not propagate smurf attacks.

- Do not reveal the netmask.

- Filter out obviously illicit or needless traffic.

- Ensure that the router will issue a reset, not silence, for denied services. A simple denial-of-service attack becomes possible if the router proxies the TCP sockets and no one is there to answer the call on the other side.

For additional insights on how to lock down your Cisco router properly, refer to the following URL, provided by Cisco: http://www.cisco.com/warp/public/707/21.html#references.

Locking Down the Firewall

Because the "rules of the firewall" tend to be something only the technical side of the house really understands, we recommend that the business side of the house create a document that defines the *business firewall policy.* This one-page document defines the services allowed into and out of the organization. Senior managers must be closely involved with the creation of this document so they understand what Internet services are flowing in and out of their e-business applications.

Once this policy is written and published, the operations team must implement and enforce the policy using the organization's standardized firewall vendor.

A last word about the Business Firewall Policy: Stick to it. If you have established a policy that denies developers the ability to telnet into the application from home, enforce it. Deviate from policy, and you risk turning your firewall into a big block of Swiss cheese, with many security holes throughout.

Creating the Demilitarized Zone (DMZ)

As discussed under Web security, all Web servers should be placed in a demilitarized zone—an area inside the firewall but located on a network separate from the corporate LAN.

You can use DMZs for other Internet-based applications, as well, such as email servers, B2B servers, and so on.

A DMZ can increase significantly the security shields for your e-business applications. When deciding whether a DMZ is right for your Web site, consider the following:

- The cost of additional devices necessary to implement a DMZ
- The decreased accessibility to an attacker
- The slight decrease in performance
- The time cost in implementing a DMZ
- The cost of additional hardware to implement a DMZ (It pales in comparison to the cost of a security breach on your corporate LAN.)

Leveraging Intrusion Detection Systems (IDS's)

An intrusion detection system (IDS) is a network-management system that gathers and analyzes information to identify possible security breaches. These may include intrusions (attacks from outside the organization) and misuse (attacks from within the organization). IDS systems are comparable to antivirus programs, which scan files for known virus patterns. An IDS program similarly scans TCP/IP packets as they stream in and out of your organization to look for common attack patterns. Suspicious activities trigger administrator alarms and other configurable responses.

Four main IDS types exist. *Network-based* systems scan the network for attacks occurring either internally or externally. *Host-based* systems screen host systems for possible attacks, including Internet-based applications running on those hosts. *Hybrid-based* systems combine the functionality of network and host-based IDS systems.

Application-based IDS systems provide application-based intrusion monitoring, which prevents, logs, and alerts administrators to any attempts at application manipulation via the browser. This product type is fairly new, and can be effective in providing yet another layer of security for your application.

Deciding where to place the IDS depends on your organization's security policy and on what you want to detect. For example, you must decide whether to place the IDS inside or outside your firewall. Placing it outside your firewall allows you to monitor all attacks directed at your network, regardless of whether they are stopped at the firewall. One drawback to this approach is that the IDS will detect far more events than an IDS inside the firewall, resulting in frequent alarms.

If the goal is to monitor the traffic your firewall lets pass, then place an IDS inside your firewall.

If resources permit, it is best to place one IDS outside and another inside your firewall. This way you can guard against every attack directed at your network and detect those that make it inside.

Host Intrusion Detection Systems

A host IDS looks at system logs for evidence of malicious or suspicious application activity in real time. It also monitors key system files for evidence of tampering. Ideally, every Internet-based application would have a host-based IDS watching the log files for any suspicious activity (including logging events the application generated).

Prior to purchasing an IDS, you should answer a few questions:

- Who will manage the IDS system?

- Who will monitor the system?

- Who will escalate potential security breaches in a timely manner?

• How much normal configuration activity—and concomitant false alarms—should you expect?

If your organization has the human resources to address these concerns, then a host-based IDS can play a superior role in guarding against malicious attacks on your Internet-based applications.

One final note: Even if you don't purchase a host-based IDS, take the initiative to write programs that scan the log files every thirty minutes to look for suspicious activity. Remember, if nobody is watching the log files, nobody is really watching.

Internal Shields of Defense

One often-overlooked safeguard to internal network security is the installation of a firewall to inhibit unauthorized internal corporate LAN traffic. The only persons who should have access to internal applications and/or database servers are the operations and database administrators. Restrict access to those systems for all other personnel and entities on the corporate LAN.

Installing an internal firewall is like placing mission-critical servers in a locked room and prohibiting anyone in the building from gaining physical access to them. The internal firewall inhibits employees from gaining unauthorized access and blocks unauthorized individuals who may gain access to your corporate LAN from reaching sensitive information housed by your application.

Chapter

Operating Systems
Security Considerations

• •

The first step in host-based security is to *harden* the operating system. That is, determine those services that must run on your host, and disable all the others. Take time to plot carefully the services you absolutely need to support the business.

The second step is to *lock down,* or secure, other areas of the operating system by limiting auxiliary entry points into the system, improving network defenses, and enabling or improving your audit trail. Document this process and repeat the procedure each time you allocate a host system for use in a production environment. The wide array of tools that can assist in locking down your operating system includes the following.

Computer Oracle and Password System (COPS)
(ftp://coast.cs.purdue.edu/pub/tools/unix/scanners/cops)
COPS checks Unix systems for common security problems, such as unsafe permissions on key files and directories.

Microsoft's Security Configuration Tool Set
(http://www.microsoft.com/windows2000/techinfo/
howitworks/security/sctoolset.asp)
The Security Configuration Tool Set allows you to configure security for a Windows 2000 system, and then perform periodic analyses of the system to ensure that the configuration remains intact or makes necessary changes over time. It is also integrated with Win-

dows administration change and configuration management to automatically configure security policies for a large number of systems in the enterprise.

Microsoft Network Security Hotfix Checker Tool

http://support.microsoft.com/default.aspx?scid=KB;EN-US;q303215&ID=KB;EN-US;q303215

The Microsoft Network Security Hotfix Checker Tool is a command-line tool administrators can use to centrally assess a computer or group of computers for the absence of security patches. You can use the tool to assess patch status for the Windows NT 4.0 and Windows 2000 operating systems and hot fixes for Internet Information Services 4.0 (IIS), Internet Information Services 5.0 (IIS), SQL Server 7.0, and SQL Server 2000 (including Microsoft Data Engine [MSDE]), and Internet Explorer 5.01 or later.

Security Administrator's Integrated Network Tool (SAINT™)

(http://www.wwdsi.com/saint)

SAINT gathers as much information about remote hosts and networks as possible by examining network services such as finger, NFS, NIS, and FTP. This information identifies the presence of various network information services, as well as potential security flaws, usually in the form of incorrectly set-up or configured network services, well-known bugs in system or network utilities, or poor or uninformed policy decisions.

Solaris™ Security Toolkit

(http://www.sun.com/security/jass)

The Solaris Security Toolkit provides a flexible and extensible mechanism to minimize, harden, and secure Solaris Operating Environment systems. Designed to simplify and automate the process of securing Solaris systems, this toolkit was developed by members of the Enterprise Engineering and Professional Services teams and is based on proven security best practices and practical customer site experience gathered over many years.

Tiger
(ftp://coast.cs.purdue.edu/pub/tools/unix/scanners/tiger)
Developed by Texas A&M University, Tiger is a set of scripts similar to COPS that scan a Unix system for security problems.

Titan
(http://www.fish.com/titan/index.html)
From http://www.fish.com/titan/lisa-paper.html:
Titan is a free, host-based security tool that can be used to improve or audit the security of a Unix system. Titan does not replace other security tools, nor does it fix or patch security bugs. Its primary purpose is to improve the security of the system it runs on by codifying as many security tricks as possible to secure an OS.

Titan improves the security of a system by:

• Cutting off entry points into the system

• Mitigating or preventing the effects of various denial-of-service attacks

• Turning on or improving the level of logging and auditing features

• Improving network and local (e.g., host level) defenses

• Assisting in programmatically defining and enforcing a system security policy

TripWire
(http://www.tripwire.com)
Tripwire is a tool that enables you to establish policies to detect intentional tampering with any system files, as well as identify the introduction of malicious software. Every production system should include this type of software because, like an IDS, it alerts you to attempted interference with your production system. This software works with Windows NT/2000, Solaris, IBM AIX, HP-UX, FreeBSD, and Linux.

Database Security Considerations

• •

One of the most ignored aspects of security is database security. Do not overlook it! The database may be tucked deep inside the firewall, but it can be a liability if you do not give it proper attention. Consider this bulletin from December 24, 2001:

> Microsoft has revealed two flaws in SQL Server 2000 and 7.0. The first flaw is a buffer overflow vulnerability that could allow an attacker to gain control of the server and reconfigure the operating system or reformat the hard drive. The second flaw is a format string vulnerability that could be exploited for a denial-of-service.—http://www.computerworld.com/storyba/0,4125,NAV47_STO66936,00.html, http:// www. microsoft.com/technet/security/bulletin/MS01-060.asp

Best Practices When Managing the Database

• •

Keep this best-practices list in mind when securing and managing the database:

- Remove the default userid and passwords for the database. (Oracle, for example, has about a dozen default accounts!)
- Disable unnecessary services on the database servers.
- Store the passwords in a locked filing cabinet, providing access only to necessary personnel.

- Make regular backups of all database files, configuration files, and stored procedures.

- Implement a backup-and-restore plan for the production database system.

- Regularly review the log files for suspicious activity. Identify the team member responsible for this.

- Maintain a written procedure for security breaches.

- Prohibit users from connecting directly to the database; instead, require them to run as a specific user or role.

- Choose strong authentication for administrative control of the database. Change the passwords twice a year.

- Confirm that the most recent security patches from the vendor have been installed properly.

- Keep credit cards and passwords hashed in the database (consider using the MD5 algorithm, or SHA-1). The idea here is that anyone who gains unauthorized access to the production database will not be able to walk away with sensitive information, because it is illegible (encrypted).

- Enforce access control with "grant" and "revoke" commands.

Security Features in SQL Server 2000

Since the December 2001 bulletin, SQL Server 2000 has been updated and re-evaluated. It currently meets U.S. government C2 security certification requirements.

Here is a guide to some key SQL Server 2000 security components.

Encryption: Network Encryption Using SSL/TLS

SQL Server 2000 now automatically supports encryption of data and other network traffic as it travels between the client and server systems on a network. Encryption strength depends on encryption capabilities authorized by the certificate installed for SQL Server and on client–server cryptographic capabilities.

The certificate selected for SQL Server must be assigned to the name of the server in the form of the fully qualified DNS server name (for example, SQLServer.Redmond.corp.Microsoft.com.). The certificate must be valid for server authentication. Log in to SQL Server as the SQL Server service account, obtain the certificate (from either an internal certificate authority or a trusted third-party provider, such as VeriSign), and install it on the server in the location suggested when you import the certificate.

SecurityAdmin

SecurityAdmin can change passwords belonging to SQL Server authentication-mode logins, except for those of sysadmin fixed-server role members, which cannot be reset. This limited capability makes SecurityAdmin a good fit for personnel in help-desk positions who do not require full-system administrator access to SQL Server.

SQL Trace

SQL Trace represents the server-side components of the auditing mechanism. Auditing capability has been added to the same mechanism that was used in SQL Server 7.0 to provide performance information about SQL Server. Performance information is still returned, as is audit information.

Each time an auditable security event occurs inside the SQL Server relational or storage engine, the event engine (SQL Trace) is notified. If a trace is currently enabled and running to capture the generated event, that event is then written to the trace file.

The foregoing information and more may be found at http:// msdn.microsoft.com.

SQL Profiler

SQL Profiler is the graphical interface utility that allows you to view the audit trace files, and then perform selected actions on those files. You can search through the files, save them to a table, and create and configure trace definitions using the user interface. SQL Profiler is a client to SQL Trace, and does not require SQL Profiler to perform a security audit.

Password Protection: Backups and Backup Media Sets

SQL Server 2000 allows you to specify a password either for an individual backup or for a backup media set. Restore of the backup is denied without the password, which enables you to protect your backups from unauthorized restores.

Unfortunately, because the data is not encrypted, a program that does not honor the Microsoft Tape Format can ignore the password and give you access to the data within the backup.

SQL Server Enterprise Manager

In SQL Server 2000, passwords for authenticated logins are always encrypted using the Windows Crypto API.

Authentication Modes

Microsoft SQL Server 2000 provides two authentication modes for securing access to the server—Windows Authentication Mode and Mixed Mode.

Application Roles

Application roles allow the database administrator to restrict user access to data, based on the application the user is running. Application roles delegate responsibility for user authentication to the application.

When an application connects to SQL Server 2000, it executes the sp_setapprole stored procedure, which examines two parameters—username and password (these parameters can be encrypted). The existing permissions assigned to the user are dropped, and the security context of the application role is assumed.

Once application roles are activated, they cannot be deactivated. The only way to return to the original security context of the user is to disconnect and reconnect to SQL Server.

Application roles work with both authentication modes, and contain no members. Users cannot be identified with application roles, because the application requests the application role's security context using a stored procedure.

Another advantage in the use of application roles is that the user running the application is audited within SQL Server 2000. In other words, application roles provide the security context within which the database object permissions are checked, but the identity of the actual user is not lost.

SQL Profiler

The SQL Profiler tool for SQL Server 2000 can save time looking through log files for suspicious activities. Use it to log a variety of events, including:

- Logins, logouts, adding users
- Changing roles and/or passwords
- Server start and stop events

Security Features in Oracle

Much of the following information is from "Database Security in Oracle8*i:* An Oracle Technical White Paper" (November 1999), which can be found in its entirety at http://otn.oracle.com/deploy/security/oracle8i/listing.htm.

Hardening Oracle

Oracle 8*i* supports a range of user authentication mechanisms, including:

- Passwords (Oracle's built-in password manager ensures strong passwords, lockout passwords, password expiration policies, prevent reuse, and so on. The Oracle password protocol also encrypts passwords being sent over the wire.)
- Digital certificates (specifically, server-to-server applications)
- Host-based authentication (by the underlying OS)
- Third party–based authentication (network authentication, smart cards, biometric devices)

In Oracle8*i,* users granted ANY privilege (such as ALTER ANY

TABLE, DROP ANY VIEW) can exercise these privileges on any appropriate object in any schema except SYS, which includes the data dictionary. This allows developers and others needing privileges on objects in multiple schemas (such as ALTER ANY TABLE) to retain that access via ANY privileges, while ensuring they do not inadvertently alter the data dictionary.

Oracle Label Security

Label-based access control provided by Oracle Label Security allows organizations to assign sensitivity labels to information, control access to data based on those labels, and ensure that data is marked with appropriate sensitivity labels.

For example, an e-business may differentiate between *company-confidential* and *public* information. It may want to share a portion of company-confidential information with partners under a confidential disclosure agreement or other legal document, or make information available to certain divisions within the company, such as finance or sales. The ability to manage labeled data provides a tremendous advantage for e-businesses, in that they are able to give the right information to the right people at the right level of secure data access.

Encrypting Oracle Passwords

For anyone securing key assets, encrypting sensitive columns in a database is just good common sense. Routinely encrypt all *credit card numbers, their expiration dates,* and *passwords.* Encrypting protects sensitive information from a variety of situations in which it could be viewed, including:

- By internal employees given authorized access to the database
- By internal employees who somehow gain unauthorized access to the database
- On unsecured printouts of tables containing sensitive information
- In SQL queries that contain confidential information (for data warehousing purposes)
- On backup tapes that can be seen when verifying the backup
- Through unsecured off-site storage of outdated backup tapes

Beware: Encrypting columns does not mean the information cannot be decrypted by cryptography tools. It is only a first line of defense against unnecessary viewing of confidential information.

Single Sign-On

Oracle Advanced Security also supports single sign-on for database users, including Kerberos and DCE. SSL-based single sign-on is also supported.

PKI Credential Management

Oracle Wallet Manager provides secure management of PKI-based user credentials.

It also manages user trustpoints—the list of root certificates that the user trusts—and is preconfigured with root certificates from PKI vendors such as VeriSign and CyberTrust.

User/Schema Separation

Oracle allows you to separate users from schemas, so that many different enterprise users can access a single, shared application schema. Instead of creating a user account in each database a user needs to access, you simply create an enterprise user inside the directory and point the user at a shared schema that other enterprise users also may access. This saves creating and managing accounts and authentication issues for each user on every database, thus lowering the cost of managing users in the enterprise.

Virtual Private Database

Oracle 9*i* contains a virtual private database (VPD) that enables data access with the assurance of physical data separation, on a per-user or per-customer basis within a single database. For example, an Internet-based online banking application can contain one database that ensures that customers see their own records only and not those of other customers.

VPD also comes with the Oracle Policy Manager, a GUI application that allows managers to apply security policies to schema objects, such as tables and views, and creates application contexts.

JDBC Thin Driver Supporting Secure Connections

Oracle9*i* includes a 100 percent Java implementation of Oracle Advanced Security encryption and integrity algorithms for use with JDBC thin clients. Thin JDBC provides the following features:

- Data encryption
- Data integrity checks
- Secure connections from thin JDBC clients to the Oracle9*i* database
- Secure connections from Oracle9*i* databases to older versions of Oracle Advanced Security–enabled databases

Preparing for a Secure Deployment

• •

When it comes to launching an e-business application and putting
it into production, do not overlook the planning and resources needed
to ensure its security. Transition is a time when security can fall
through the cracks. Here is a checklist to guarantee a successful and
secure deployment:

- Plan for the hand-off from QA to production personnel.

- Document all configuration information for software and
  database, including tables that must be prepopulated. This
  should include application-related userid/password, database
  administrator privileges, and so on.

- Train operational team members on this new application.

- Train help desk personnel (tier1 and tier2 support).

- Assign roles to the help desk to better manage user accounts.

The way you handle security during the hand-off phase of launching
a new application sets the tone for operational and help desk personnel. Do it right, and you raise the expectations of all team members. After all, if you have properly designed your Internet-based
application in a secure manner, and it is going to be effective in gen-
erating revenue for the organization, it may be in production for
many years to come. Why not invest some extra effort to deploy the
application securely?

Chapter

11

Securing the Production Environment

• •

The secure launch of your application is just the beginning. Everything up to this point has been a rehearsal, but once your application enters the real world it instantly becomes a target.

All new software launches have a few hiccups before the application begins to run smoothly. Once it settles down, one or more operations team members typically take over the task of monitoring the application. How well they respond to problems depends on their training and awareness. Make sure up front that they have the tools for managing a potential crisis.

Watching the Security Bulletins

• •

Consider a scenario in which an operations team member receives an alert describing the latest worm racing like wildfire through the Internet. Because her decisions will immediately impact the e-business application running in production, she needs bulletproof standard operating procedures (SOPs) to manage the crisis. The following questions should frame the SOPs to define the problem quickly and determine a solution:

- Does this security alert affect our systems?

- Should I take the application offline until this is investigated?

- Is this an operating system– or Web server– or application security–related bug? Are there patches available? Where do I get them? What "side effects" do they have?

• How can I tell whether our systems have been affected? (What text do I look for in the Web server log files?)

• Who do I contact to check out the application?

Team manager should keep these points in mind:

• Acknowledge that this team member is on the firing line.

• Help whenever you can.

• Recognize that this person is not perfect, and may make mistakes or misjudgments.

• Recognize that the e-business application may experience downtime, but a bit of downtime is better than a security breach.

Managing Operating-System Security Patches

It is difficult to make good decisions under pressure. If they are prepared, your team members can stay poised. Create standard operating procedures for each contingency. If you stay directed, you can stay calm even in the middle of a storm.

Standard operations manuals should be structured as shown in the following tables. Clearly, having all this information readily available can save many minutes of downtime.

Table 11-1. Operating Systems SOP Manual Structure				
Hostname	Operating System	OS Version	Physical Location	Owner
Fido	Solaris	7.0	Server room	Jon
Bart	Windows	2000 SP2	Server room	Tim

Monitoring Log Files for Suspicious Activity

Know how to quickly log onto suspect systems. Understand the tools for wading through the log files. (Refer to the section "Tools to Help Monitor Security Logs" in Chapter 6 of this book.)

Table 11-2. Web-Server SOP Manual Structure

Hostname	Web Server Type	Web Server Version	Physical Location	Owner
Fido	Apache	1.3	Server room	Jon
Bart	IIS	5.x	Server room	Tim

Table 11-3. Internet-Based Application SOP Manual Structure

Hostname	Internet-Based Application	Application Version	Physical Location	Owner
Fido	Cruises For Leisure Time	1.5	Server room	Jon
Bart	B2B For U	1.7	Server room	Tim

Table 11-4. Application Server SOP Manual Structure

Hostname	Application Server	Application Version	Physical Location	Owner
Fido	WebLogic	5.x	Server room	Jon
Bart	WebLogic	6.x	Server room	Tim

Table 11-5. Database Security Server SOP Manual Structure

Hostname	Application Server	Application Version	Physical Location	Owner
Fido	Oracle	Oracle8*i*	Server room	Jon
Bart	SQL Server	2000 sp1	Server room	Tim

Chapter

12

Quality Assurance (QA)

Testing is critical to verify that the requirements of the application are present and functioning correctly. The basic testing of an application (finding and removing defects) only begins the process of mitigating risks. The job of quality assurance extends well beyond the QA department; it involves the scrutiny of all teams within the organization. Quality applications depend on meaningful communication among teams.

Above and beyond the routine functional testing of application is a methodology we call *security verification*. It probes the application for security defects (as opposed to functional defects).

In probing an application to see how well it holds up against real-world vulnerabilities, Security Verification first scrutinizes the system by:

- *Understanding* the security requirements addressed in the architecture and design
- *Designing* verification suites
- *Coding* verification suites
- *Injecting* the verification suites against the system

Benefits of Security Verification

An application that stands up to the scrutiny of a security verification demonstrates a high level of certainty over a range of security functions. A successful verification should confirm that:

- the application has been coded securely and is resilient to common attacks (buffer overflows and the like)
- the authentication mechanisms of the application are working correctly
- the access control mechanisms of the application function accurately

Sample Security Verification Suite

Here is a sample template for designing a security verification suite for a Web-site login scenario.

Scenario: User goes to a Web page, enters a username and password and clicks on the login button.

Background: Interview the development team to generate a clear understanding of the architecture and design of the security modules in the application.

Design: Design the verification suite to drive the login scenario (including information gathered from the developers).

Code: To code the verification suite, write a script (in an HTTP-based programming language) to orchestrate and drive this scenario.

Apply: Execute the verification suite against the target application.

Results: Compare the expected results with the actual results. Document and analyze all findings.

Action Items: Have the developers fix the broken pieces and schedule a retest of this scenario.

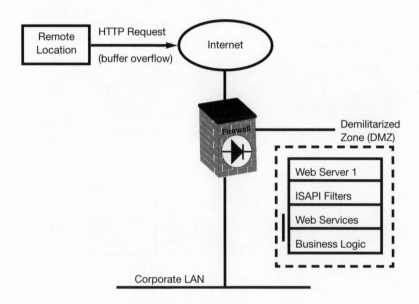

Security Verification Suite Buffer Overflow

Figure 12–1. A security verification suite attempting a buffer overflow against the Internet-based application. Notice that the buffer overflow is injected remotely over the public Internet and could be directed to attack any layer (authentication, access control, Web services, and/or business logic) within the application.

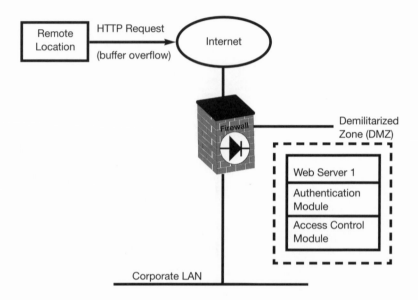

Security Verification Suite Session Playback

Figure 12–2. A security verification suite that tries to replay a previously recorded authenticated session against the Internet-based application. This replay could ask to retrieve a bank balance or book a travel reservation.

The Wisdom in Third-Party Application Security Audits

● ●

Hiring an experienced application security auditor to test your Internet-based application helps to uncover and manage known and unknown risks. Just as the quality assurance (QA) division is responsible for verifying that all business requirements have been implemented in the application, a third-party security auditor can verify that all security requirements are in place and working effectively.

Ideally, companies should perform an architecture-and-design audit during these phases of the project. A subsequent implementation audit should take place once the software is ready for beta. Even if your Internet-based application is already running in production, it is never too late to conduct an application security audit. Your application is likely to contain a number of vulnerabilities that have not been exploited yet—or they *have* been exploited, but you do not know about it!

An application security audit is a proactive way to protect your Internet-based applications. (Refer to Appendix J of this book, "Components of a Riskology Application Security Audit.")

Guiding Principles

• Start risk management of the e-business application as early as possible, and continue managing risk during the life cycle of the application.

• Have an objective third-party expert test your application security shields. Team members intimately involved with the application cannot always identify security errors and/or omissions in their own work. An extra pair of eyes and ears almost always pays off in managing security for any e-business application.

Social Engineering

• •

The single weakest link in e-business security is not firewalls, not host systems, not applications. It is the *people*—the man or woman sitting behind your reception desk or answering the phone from the help desk.

Kevin Mitnick, one of the most notorious hackers in Internet history, was not a master of cryptography or a genius at cracking passwords. He was a personable guy with a nice smile, who was brilliant at engaging people's trust, and so getting them to hand over unauthorized information that enabled him to access corporate systems.

Countermeasures

• •

The best defense against attacks by crafty, sweet-talking social engineers is education. Schedule twice-yearly security-awareness training for *all* personnel. Train your staff to protect your company's key assets by keeping their lips sealed, desks cleared, and all sensitive information shredded.

Security-awareness training provides a number of benefits:

- It trains the Help Desk to be helpful without giving out sensitive information over the phone.

- It alerts personnel to the strategies of social engineers trying to gain unauthorized information.

- It demonstrates the importance of shredding all sensitive hard-copy documents.

- It stresses the importance of strong passwords.
- It directs employees to keep their desks clear of sensitive documents overnight.
- It highlights the top security mistakes IT personnel typically make.
- It emphasizes the value of the company's IT assets (tangible and intangible) and the role employees play in protecting their own futures.

Table 14–1 lists common social-engineering tactics and prevention strategies.

Table 14–1. Social-Engineering Tactics and Prevention Strategies

Area of Risk	Social Engineering Tactic	Countermeasure
Help Desk	Impersonation and persuasion	Train help-desk employees never to give out passwords or other confidential information over the telephone. All employees should be assigned a PIN specific to help-desk support.
Building entrance	Unauthorized physical access	Tight badge security, employee training, and security officers present

Area of Risk	Social Engineering Tactic	Countermeasure
Office	Shoulder surfing	Never type in passwords with anyone else present. (Or, if you must, do it *quickly!*)
Office	Wandering through halls looking for open offices	Wandering through halls looking for open offices Require all guests to be escorted. Keep phone closets, server rooms, and the like locked at all times and keep updated inventory on equipment.
Dumpsters	Dumpster diving	Keep all trash in secured, monitored areas. Shred important data. Erase magnetic media.
Office	Stealing sensitive documents	Mark documents as confidential and keep documents locked.

Appendix A: Senior Manager's Security Checklist

❑ Create a budget specifically for IT security

❑ Create a document that lists all e-business applications in order of importance to the company (in terms of risk and/or revenue-generating capacity). Review this document with the company's chief officers and board of directors. Establish consensus upon the prioritized order. Based on this document, budget and schedule an application security audit for the first three Internet-based applications on the list.

❑ Schedule a monthly meeting with the Security Council to review high-level Internet-based risks and how they are being addressed. Keep a log of initiatives, accomplishments, and year-to-date security expenses. (In the absence of a security director, spend time with your company's directors, operations manager, and technical leaders to assess security status.)

❑ Schedule and budget twice-yearly security-awareness training for the entire organization. Track the return on investment (ROI) as perceived by others in the organization, including officers of the company.

❑ Ensure that the company's enterprise-wide policies and procedures are in order and are being adhered to.

❑ Schedule quarterly meetings with the board of directors and all officers of the company to share ongoing status of the managed risks.

❑ Amend the annual performance review to include
  • a review of specific security concerns reported to each employee's manager
  • an evaluation of adherence to company policies and procedures

- incentives for employees to alert the company to specific security concerns or challenges

❏ Measure the ROI for all security-related initiatives. Share the results of those investments with your clients, board of directors, and strategic alliance partners to promote full trust in your e-business applications.

❏ Required reading: *Secrets and Lies: Digital Security in a Networked World,* by Bruce Schneier. (Refer to the Annotated Bibliography at the end of this book for complete publication information.)

Appendix B: Security Director's Checklist

❑ Review senior management's security overview of the company's prioritized e-business applications. Report to senior management any perceived discrepancies or recommendations.

❑ Schedule and meet with as many people in the organization as possible to discuss security. Create an executive summary and report your findings to senior management. (This data should inform other initiatives, such as security awareness training and the implementation of specific security measures.)

❑ Own the security policies and procedures document. Ensure that it is being complied with on a daily basis. Update it as necessary.

❑ Schedule quarterly meetings with all company officers to assess and report on all security related risks being managed.

❑ Required reading: *Secrets and Lies: Digital Security in a Networked World,* by Bruce Schneier; *Hacking Exposed,* by Joel Scambray and Mike Shema; subscribe to *Information Security* magazine. Refer to the Annotated Bibliography at the end of this book for complete publication information.

Appendix C: Director's and Program Manager's Checklist

· ·

If there is no security director in your company, you are officially responsible for implementing all checklists for that role.

❑ Ensure that all security policies and procedures are in place and conform to acceptable standards. Assess the level of your personnel's compliance with the policies and procedures document. Note your findings and review them in all your direct reports, including those to senior management.

❑ Required reading: *Secrets and Lies: Digital Security in a Networked World,* by Bruce Schneier; *Hacking Exposed,* by Joel Scambray and Mike Shema; subscribe to *Information Security* magazine. Refer to the Annotated Bibliography at the end of this book for complete publication information.

❑ Ask yourself, "What am I doing to improve the security of the company's Internet-based applications?" Document your actions (including items implemented from this checklist) and save for your annual review.

Appendix D: Operations Manager's Checklist

❏ Ensure that all security policies and procedures are in place and conform to acceptable standards. Assess personnel compliance with the policies and procedures document. Note your findings and review them in all of direct reports, including those to senior management.

❏ Closely monitor all major security vulnerability email alert services.

❏ Assign at least three of your reports to subscribe to all major security vulnerability email alerts. Assign a responsible person, on a rotating basis (per monthly usually works best), to be on call and on alert for any severe alerts that are published. Assigning three people helps in the case of vacations, sick days, attrition, and so on.

❏ Meet with your team once a month to discuss security of the company's Internet-based applications.

❏ Required reading:
   Secrets and Lies: Digital Security in a Networked World, by Bruce Schneier
   Hacking Exposed, by Joel Scambray and Mike Shema
   Building Internet Firewalls (2d edition), by Elizabeth D. Zwicky
   Information Security magazine (subscribe)
   Refer to the Annotated Bibliography at the end of this book for complete publication information.

❏ Ask yourself, "What am I doing to improve the security of the company's Internet-based applications?" Document your actions (including items implemented from this checklist) and save for your annual review.

Appendix E: Operations Team Member's Checklist

❑ Ensure that you understand and are adhering to the security policies and procedures in place. Assess personnel compliance with the policies and procedures document. Note your findings and review them in all direct reports, including those to senior management.

❑ Closely monitor all major security vulnerability email alert services.

❑ Required reading:

Secrets and Lies: Digital Security in a Networked World, by Bruce Schneier

Hacking Exposed, by Joel Scambray and Mike Shema

Building Internet Firewalls (2d edition), by Elizabeth D. Zwicky

Practical Unix and Internet Security, by Simson Garfinkel and Gene Spafford

Intrusion Detection, by Rebecca Gurley Bace

Information Security magazine (subscribe)

Refer to the Annotated Bibliography at the end of this book for complete publication information.

❑ Ask yourself, "What am I doing to improve the security of the company's Internet-based applications?" Document your actions (including items implemented from this checklist) and save for your annual review.

Appendix F: Technical Leader's Checklist

❏ Ensure that security is an intimate part of each and every application you are chartered to build!

❏ Meet with your team quarterly to discuss security issues relating to company Internet-based applications.

❏ Monitor all major security vulnerability email alert services.

❏ Required reading:

Secrets and Lies: Digital Security in a Networked World, by Bruce Schneier

Hacking Exposed, by Joel Scambray and Mike Shema

Building Internet Firewalls (2d edition), by Elizabeth D. Zwicky

Practical Unix and Internet Security, by Simson Garfinkel and Gene Spafford

Writing Secure Code, by Michael Howard and David LeBlanc

Building Secure Software, by John Viega and Gary McGraw

Information Security magazine (subscribe)

Refer to the Annotated Bibliography at the end of this book for complete publication information.

❏ Ask yourself, "What am I doing to improve the security of the company's Internet-based applications?" Document your actions (including items implemented from this checklist) and save for your annual review.

Appendix G: Technical Team Member's Checklist

❑ Adhere to all security initiative that the technical leader puts into practice.

❑ Required reading:
Secrets and Lies: Digital Security in a Networked World, by Bruce Schneier.
Hacking Exposed, by Joel Scambray and Mike Shema
Building Internet Firewalls (2d edition), by Elizabeth D. Zwicky
Practical Unix and Internet Security, by Simson Garfinkel and Gene Spafford
Writing Secure Code, by Michael Howard and David LeBlanc
Building Secure Software, by John Viega and Gary McGraw
Information Security magazine (subscribe)
Refer to the Annotated Bibliography at the end of this book for complete publication information.

❑ Ask yourself, "What am I doing to improve the security of the company's Internet-based applications?" Document your actions (including items implemented from this checklist) and save for your annual review.

Appendix H: Sample Web-Site Security Policy

Personnel

Access Levels

1. The public: Read-only access to all URLs with the exception of the /security directory.
2. Company employees: Read-only access to all parts of the site, including the /security directory.
3. Developers: Access to create, modify and delete all files in the *staging* document tree.
4. Administrators: Access to modify the Web-server host configurations on *staging* as well as *production*. This includes starting and stopping the host machine.

Authorization Procedure

For access levels 3 and 4, personnel must obtain written authorization from the director of security.

Revocation of Authorization

For access levels 2 through 4, authorization may be revoked without warning at the discretion of the director of security.

Access Privileges

Local Login

Local (console) login to the production Web server is allowed for system and site administrators only. Logins are for the purpose of site maintenance only.

Network Login

Only administrators may use Windows Terminal Services to access the machine remotely. This is for maintenance/monitoring purposes only. Make sure strong passwords are used and that they are changed twice a year.

Web-Site Installation

All components comprising the application can be installed by site administrators after at least two members of the Quality Assurance team have validated the staging components.

Network Services

Web

The Web site will provide Web services via port 443 (HTTPS).

FTP

Incoming and outgoing FTP is used only to update Web components. This service should be disabled when not in use.

Other Services

The Web host provides no other network services.

Maintenance

The site should be accessible twenty-four hours a day, seven days a week, except for a nightly scheduled two-hour maintenance period between 3 a.m. and 5 a.m. System administrators should be prepared to switch to a backup server in a timely manner in case the primary server develops hardware or software issues.

Backup

A complete backup of the Web-server host will be done weekly, and incremental backups daily.

Restore

A complete restore of the Web server will be performed twice a year. This scheduled maintenance will be coordinated by the director of security.

Off-Site Storage

A complete archive of the Web site will be stored in a secured, off-site storage facility once a month.

Appendix I: Sample Security Policy and Procedure Outline

Legal Documents
  Nondisclosure
  Employee Agreement
  Policies and Procedures
  Employee Acknowledgment Form
  Drug Testing
  Background Check

Employee Usage of Company Resources and Intellectual Property
  Boot-time Passwords
  Strong Passwords
  Twice-yearly Change of Passwords
  20-Minute Screen Lock
  Weekly Backup of Company Information
  Secure Email Usage
  Internet Usage
  Shredding of Sensitive Information
  Marking Confidential Documents
  Clear Desk Policy
  Company Door Lock
  Employee Badges
  Handling Visitors
  Security Awareness Training

Administrative Policies and Procedures for Computing Resources
  Twice-yearly Inventory of IT Assets
  Machine Configurations
  Fire Extinguishers

Uninterruptible Power Supply (UPS)
Computing/Operational Manuals
Nightly/Weekly Backups
Bi-annual Restore
Monthly Offsite Storage
Password Backup and Restore
Secure Server Room
Software/CD Storage and Checkout
Library Checkout Procedures
Hard Document Safe Storage

Network Security

Access to Corporate LAN
Business Firewall Policy
Technical Firewall Implementation
Router
Remote Access

Handling Security Incidents

First-tier Forensics
Crisis Communications Procedures
Properly Documenting the Incident

Appendix J: Components of a Riskology Application Security Audit

To ensure the integrity of a company's Web applications, Riskology, Inc., offers Application Security Certification (ASC^{SM}), a state-of-the-art, uncompromising assessment of IT security that sets a new industry standard. The ASC product measures the security posture of a Web application, as well as the environment in which it functions. Its demanding review includes an audit of the architecture, design, and implementation of the software and provides an in-depth evaluation of the network securing the application (internally and externally). In addition, Riskology's ASC contains a security-code review, which examines those components of an application that handle security functions such as authentication, access control, and audit trails. The ASC completes its test of the system by rigorously attempting to gain unauthorized access to various components of the application.

Riskology's application security assessment generates a comprehensive report that provides in-depth understanding of the Web environment's exposure to attack, and profiles the security challenges involved in developing or deploying a Web application. The resulting "Application Risk Assessment Report" details any existing risks, documenting severity, the personnel responsible, the cost/benefit of resolution, and current status.

Once Riskology's ASC program has identified and documented an application's vulnerabilities, it offers specific recommendations to resolve any existing or potential security issues. Subsequent resolution may be addressed either by the client or by one of Riskology's strategic alliances. Upon resolution of the identified vulnerabilities, Riskology will perform a rigorous second audit of the application to ensure that appropriate steps have been taken to minimize or eliminate any current or potential security risks. On successful completion of the second audit, Riskology issues an Application Security Certificate^{SM,} which completes the process.

By receiving Riskology's ASC, a company can confidently demonstrate to its employees, clients, partners, investors, and strategic allies that it has taken the steps necessary to ensure the integrity, availability, confidentiality, and security of their Internet-based applications.

Glossary of Technical Terms

access control

The process of limiting access to information to authorized subjects or objects. Access control works hand-in-hand with authentication. (That is, access control relies on the fact that the entity has been authenticated already).

application

Any specific task, as billing or inventory, to be performed by a computer; a program for performing such task.

application programming interface (API)

A well-defined interface published for any to use but abstracting the details of the implementation; the specific method prescribed by a computer operating system or by an application program by which a programmer writing an application program can make requests of the operating system or another application.

audit trail

An automated or manual set of records providing documentary evidence of user transactions, used to aid in tracing system activities, access violations, and so on.

authentication

The act of identifying or providing assurance regarding the identity of a subject or object—for example, ensuring that a particular user is who he claims to be. Internet-based applications provide authentication mechanisms in the form of a username and password. Much stronger forms of authentication exist, such as digital certificates.

backup
The activity of copying files or databases so that they will be preserved in case of equipment failure or other catastrophe.

bastion hosts
The only host computer on the Internet that a company allows to be addressed directly from the public network, designed to screen the rest of its network from security exposure.

best practices
Applying proven standards recognized by the community at large.

bill of rights
A list of the rights and freedoms assumed to be essential to a group of people.

conditions-of-use policy
A policy that states all legal implications of using a particular Internet-based application.

confidentiality
When used in reference to an Internet-based application, ensuring that information is disclosed only to authorized subjects or objects (i.e., individuals, computer processes, and the like).

configuration management (CM)
The detailed recording and updating of information that describes an enterprise's computer systems and networks, including all hardware and software components. Such information typically includes versions and updates that have been applied to installed software packages and the locations and network addresses of hardware devices.

cryptography
The science of information security. Includes techniques such as microdots, merging words with images, and other ways to hide information in storage or transit. Most often associated with scrambling

plaintext into ciphertext (a process called *encryption*), and then back again (known as *decryption*).

demilitarized zone (DMZ)
A computer host or small network inserted as a "neutral zone" between a company's private network and the outside public network to prevent outside users from gaining direct access to a server that stores company data.

denial of service (DoS)
An attack or incident in which a user or organization is deprived of the services of a resource they would normally expect to have. Can destroy programming and files in a computer system. May be costly to the target person or company in terms of time and money.

digital certificate
An electronic "credit card" that establishes your credentials when conducting business or other transactions on the Web. Issued by a certification authority (CA), and contains name, serial number, expiration dates, a copy of the certificate holder's public key and the digital signature of the certificate-issuing authority so that a recipient can verify the certificate.

domain name system (DNS)
The way that Internet domain names are located and translated into Internet protocol addresses; a meaningful and easy-to-remember "handle" for an Internet address.

e-business
electronic business transactions (buying and selling, servicing customers, and collaborating with business partners) that occur via the Internet.

encryption
An electronic digital code added to data being sent over the public network to prevent its unauthorized detection, use, and so on.

finger

A program that provides the name associated with an email address. May also reveal whether the user is logged in at their system, their most recent logon session, and possibly other information, depending on the data maintained about users on that computer.

firewall

A set of related programs located at a network gateway server that protects the resources of a private network from users from other networks.

file transfer protocol (FTP)

An application protocol that uses the Internet's TCP/IP protocols; the simplest way to exchange files between computers on the Internet.

hacking

An attempt to break into a computer system.

hardware

The mechanical, magnetic, and electronic design, structure, and devices of a computer or computer system.

heavyweight Web site

An e-commerce Web site "heavy" in the sense that it is sophisticated. It stores sensitive information, processes credit-card information, conveys basic information, and keeps track of user preferences.

high availability

When used in reference to an Internet-based application, the timely, reliable access to data and information services for authorized users; "up time" for users.

host based

Concerned with the host system, as opposed to the network.

hypertext transfer protocol over secure socket layer (HTTPS; HTTP over SSL)
A Web protocol developed by Netscape and built into its browser that encrypts and decrypts user page requests as well as pages returned by the Web server. HTTPS is really just the use of Netscape's secure socket layer (SSL) as a sublayer under its regular HTTP application layering.

hypertext
Information stored in a computer and specially organized so that related items, as in separate documents, are linked and readily accessible.

information technology (IT)
All forms of technology used to create, store, exchange, and use information in its various forms (business data, voice conversations, still images, motion pictures, multimedia presentations, and other forms, including those not yet conceived).

integrity
When used in reference to an Internet-based application, ensuring that information is changed only by authorized subjects or objects (individuals, computer processes, and the like).

Internet
An extensive computer network made up of thousands of other, smaller business, academic, and government networks.

intrusion detection systems (IDS)
Type of network security management system that gathers and analyzes information to identify possible security breaches, including intrusions (attacks from outside the organization) and misuse (attacks from within the organization).

Internet protocol (IP)
The method by which data is sent from one computer to another on

the Internet. Each computer (known as a *host*) on the Internet has at least one IP address that uniquely distinguishes it from all other computers on the Internet

Internet Protocol Security (IPSEC)
A developing standard for security at the network processing layer of network communication.

Java
A programming language expressly designed for use in the distributed environment of the Internet.

lightweight Web site
An informational Web site, lightweight in the sense that its basic purpose is to convey information, not to collect and store information.

local area network (LAN)
A group of computers and associated devices that share a common communications line and typically share the resources of a single processor or server within a small geographic area (for example, an office building). Usually the server stores applications and data shared by multiple computer users.

locked down
A term implying that the machine or operating system or application has some inherent measure of security.

login
The procedure used to gain access to an operating system or application, usually in a remote computer.

MAX connections
The greatest number of connections allowable at any one time.

middleweight Web site
A scaled-down Web site, middleweight in the sense that it is somewhat

more sophisticated than a lightweight Web site. Specifically, one or more database machines exist that store some sensitive information (userid and password, credit-card information, and so on), but not as much as a heavyweight Web site.

network file system (NFS)
An application that lets a computer user view and optionally store and update files on a remote computer.

operating system (OS)
The software that sits just above the hardware; the program that manages all the other programs in a computer.

protocol
The special set of rules that end points in a telecommunication connection follow when they communicate.

privacy policy
A statement designed to notify Web-site users exactly how the confidentiality of their personal information will or will not be protected.

privilege
The level of operator permission or authority.

quick restore
Ability to restore a backup tape rapidly.

restoring
Retrieval of backup files.

return on investment (ROI)
The amount of "return," usually in the form of profit or cost saving, that results from a given use of money in an enterprise.

router
A network device that helps direct network traffic into and out of your organization.

secure shell (SSH)
Sometimes known as secure socket shell, a Unix-based command interface and protocol for securely gaining access to a remote computer. SSH commands are encrypted and secure in several ways.

server
The central computer in a network to which other computers or terminals are connected; shared programs, files, and databases are stored on the server.

session replay
The process of recording all HTTP requests and responses from a valid application session for later playback (to gain unauthorized access to the application).

single sign-on
The ability to log into one application and gain access to a number of other applications without logging in again.

social engineering
A nontechnical type of intrusion that relies heavily on human interaction and often involves influencing others within an organization to break normally secure procedures.

software
The programs, routines, and the like used in a computer or computer system.

secure socket layer (SSL)
The layer that sits just below your protocol that manages the security of a message transmission on the Internet that uses encryption and digital certificates.

spoofing
The interception, alteration, and retransmission of data in an attempt to fool the recipient.

transmission control protocol (TCP)
A set of rules (protocols) used along with the Internet protocol (IP) to send data in the form of message units between computers over the Internet.

Trojan horse
A computer program containing hidden, typically damaging, functions.

Unix
An operating system that originated at Bell Labs in 1969 as an interactive time-sharing system. Unix became the first open or standard operating system that could be improved or enhanced by anyone.

virtual private network (VPN)
A private data network that maintains privacy through the use of a tunneling protocol and security procedures; involves encrypting and decrypting.

virus
An unauthorized, disruptive set of instructions placed in a computer program that leaves copies of itself in other programs and disks.

World Wide Web (www)
A group of Internet sites connected by means of hypertext, providing access to images and sound in addition to text.

worm
A computer program that invades computers on a network, typically replicating itself to prevent deletion, which interferes with the host computer's operation.

Annotated Bibliography

This selected bibliography is designed to provide a working knowledge for securing Internet-based applications.

Books

Garfinkel, Simson, and Gene Spafford. *Practical Unix and Internet Security.* 2d ed. Sebastopol, CA: O'Reilly & Associates, 1996. A classic book on host and network security.

Howard, Michael. *Designing Secure Web-Based Applications for Microsoft Windows 2000.* Redmond, WA: Microsoft Press, 2000. A broad examination of key topics relating to Web-based security for Windows development, including .NET insights.

Howard, Michael, and David Leblanc. *Writing Secure Code.* Redmond, WA: Microsoft Press, 2002. Excellent how-to guide. The '90s brought us Howard's *Writing Solid Code* and *Code Complete;* now we have the blueprints for writing *secure* code.

Scambray, Joel, and Mike Shema. *Hacking Exposed: Web Applications.* Np, Osborne McGraw-Hill, 2002. The best-selling, in-depth description of how hackers penetrate corporate networks.

Schneier, Bruce. *Secrets and Lies: Digital Security in a Networked World.* New York: John Wiley & Sons, 2000. A must-read for the entire organization. Describes the landscape of systems and threats, the technologies used to protect and intercept data, and strategies for proper implementation of security systems.

Stein, Lincoln D. *Web Security: A Step-by-Step Reference Guide.* Menlo Park, CA: Addison-Wesley, 1998. Lincoln Stein is known for his early efforts in addressing security-related issues for Web sites. His pioneer work started out with the World Wide Web Security FAQ located at http://www.w3.org/Security/Faq/www-security-faq.html.

Viega, John, and Gary McGraw. *Building Secure Software: How to Avoid Security Problems the Right Way.* Menlo Park, CA: Addison-Wesley,

2002. Excellent look at writing secure code from a risk-management perspective. The book presents ten guiding principles, highlighting the most important objectives to keep in mind for building secure software.

Zwicky, D. Elizabeth, et al. *Building Internet Firewalls.* 2d ed. Sebastopol, CA: O'Reilly & Associates, 2000. An invaluable and classic security text. It covers far more than the title suggests, including policies, protocols, and overall security for the organization.

Periodicals

Information Security magazine, http://www.infosecuritymag.com.